MARY FORD

QUICK & EASY CAKES

MARY FORD

AUTHOR

Colour backdrops supplied by Robert Horne Paper Company Limited, Eastleigh, Hampshire.

Typesetting by Avant Mode Limited, Bournemouth.

ISBN 0 946429 42 1

Mary Ford's expertise and innovative skills are well known in the cake-decorating world and she has an unsurpassed reputation for cake-artistry. She has been teaching the art of cake decoration for three decades. In that time she has shared her expertise with thousands of students. Now devoting her time entirely to writing, her books have become international bestsellers bringing her work to an ever-increasing audience.

However, Mary has never lost her personal touch and it is her endearing warmth that everyone remembers. Former students still seek her out and she always finds time to personally answer the many letters she receives. It is this warmth and her enthusiasm for her craft that shines through Mary's books.

As always, Mary's husband, Michael, has been closely involved in this book. He is both the photographer and executive editor.

MARY FORD

CONTENTS

Note: when making any of the recipes in this book, follow one set of measurements only as they are not interchangeable.

INTRODUCTION

In this 'Quick and Easy' book you will find ninety-eight original designs which are both easy to make – and at the same time stunningly effective. Most of the cakes require little expertise, but the finished product is impressive. The designs are suitable for all occasions and levels of skill. The book is intended for experienced cake-decorators who are looking for new inspiration, or beginners who want to start this absorbing hobby.

I have deliberately created designs that do not need complicated and time consuming techniques such as built-up layers of over-piping, delicate sugar flowers, or run-out work. Instead, I have chosen easy methods with stunning colour combinations and unusual designs to add impact. The step-by-step photographs show clearly every stage of the decorating process.

More time can be saved by the use of readily available items such as silk flowers and artificial decorations. Doll's bodies have been dressed to make them suitable for a variety of occasions. Simple techniques like embossing with a button create an intriguing design that looks highly professional. Using stencils and royal icing creates intricate patterns with a minimum of work. Whilst piping gel makes an artist out of the most inexperienced cake-decorator.

The book contains imaginative designs for all interests and occasions. The ideas range from christening, wedding, anniversary, retirement, Christmas and birthday cakes. I have included traditional designs and novelties. The unusual zodiac cakes, for instance, are suitable for everyone, young or old. There are cakes for all ages from the newest arrival to a grandparent.

Tried and tested basic recipes are given at the front of the book with appropriate quantities and cooking times for different sized cakes. I have included recipes for sugarpaste, royal icing and almond paste but these can be purchased if time is short.

Whilst the cakes are suitable for all levels of skill, beginners will find it worthwhile reading through the preliminary pages which demonstrate the preparation and coating of cakes. This preparation will ensure the best possible finish thereby making decorating easier. Instructions are also given for other basic steps such as making piping bags and templates. My Hints and Tips are also included and contains helpful advice for better results.

I do hope that you will enjoy making the new designs in this book.

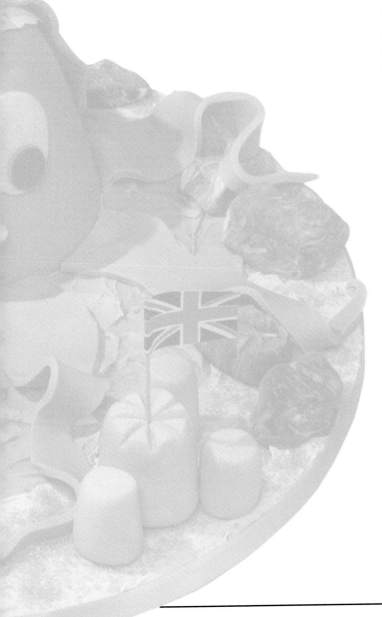

EQUIPMENT

Equipment should be chosen with care. When purchasing new equipment, always buy the best available as this will not chip, rust or bend, and should last a lifetime with careful use. Wherever possible, wooden spoons and plastic bowls should be set aside for decorating use as otherwise icing may be tainted. Stainless steel can be used, but other metals will discolour the icing and should be avoided. A food mixer is useful for mixing cakes, coverings and coatings. You will probably already have measuring jugs, nylon sieves, etc. in your home. Always ensure that equipment is kept scrupulously clean and free from grease.

Having the correct equipment to hand makes cake decorating much easier but it is possible to improvise from equipment already found in the kitchen. A turntable, for instance, can be made from an upturned cake tin or plate, although this will not support a heavy fruit cake. A good turntable will support a heavy cake and turn easily when in use. It should have a non-slip base and a minimum diameter of 23cm (9").

A good quality, smooth and heavy rolling pin about 45cm (18") will be needed for rolling out pastes, and nylon spacers can be useful for ensuring an even thickness. Stainless steel palette knives with firm blades will be needed for mixing in colour and for coating cakes, and a straight edge rigid plastic or stainless steel rule will be required for smoothing buttercream or royal icing. Purpose-made side scrapers make patterning the side of a cake easier. Scrapers are usually made of plastic and should be fairly rigid.

Instructions for making a greaseproof paper piping bag are given on page 30 and this is recommended for all icing. Piping tubes, plastic or metal, are readily available and the tube numbers are indicated ( ) throughout the text. Tubes should always be thoroughly washed immediately after use to prevent the icing hardening inside.

WHITWORTHS

For over 100 years Whitworths have been sourcing premium quality ingredients from around the world for people to use in baking and decorating cakes.

Dried Fruits, sourced from as far away as Australia and America, fall into two categories:

Dried Vine Fruits – Currants, Sultanas and Raisins are all made by taking whole bunches of Grapes from the grapevine and laying them out to dry naturally under the warmth of the sun. The resultant Dried Fruit is a source of minerals (including Calcium, Iron and Copper) and Vitamins, particularly A and B groups.

Dried Tree Fruits, are equally as nutritious as the Dried Vine Fruits. An extensive range is available offering the old baking favourites such as Dates, either sugar rolled ready chopped or whole, and Figs. Dried Plums, commonly referred to as Prunes, Apricots, Apple Rings, Pears and Peaches can be added in place of traditional Vine Fruits, to bake interesting cakes. Dried Banana Chips are great for decorating cakes or sprinkling over ice cream and puddings.

Glacé Fruits are additional favourite store cupboard ingredients. Whitworths source only the finest Bigarreaux Cherries, grown in the Provence region of France and acknowledged to be the finest Glacé Cherries in the world.

Nuts play an important role in homebaking. In the past, Nuts tended to be used for their crunchy texture and flavour alone, but now they are recognised for their high nutritional value. Nuts are rich in Protein as well as Calcium, Vitamin B and Iron. All Nuts must be stored in a cool dry place to ensure that they do not become oily or rancid.

The most popular Nut for baking is the Sweet Almond. Sweet Almonds are available whole blanched, flaked, chopped or ground and are ideal in cakes, biscuits and puddings.

Hazelnuts, sometimes called Filberts, are closely related to Cob Nuts. Either chopped or ground they can be added to cakes, pastries or puddings. The brown skins can be removed from Hazelnuts although the skins do look attractive when the whole nuts are used as a decoration.

Chopped mixed Nuts are handy for cake decorating and creating a crunchy texture for sauces and over ice cream.

Desiccated Coconut is produced by shredding the whitemeat of coconut and leaving it to dry in the sun. It can be toasted or coloured and used to flavour or decorate cakes or biscuits.

Using only the finest quality Almonds and Icing Sugar, Whitworths produce both Golden and White Marzipan to provide cake makers with an easy to use product for applying to cakes or modelling.

Whitworths were the innovators in the Ready-To-Roll Icing market, creating a delicious fondant Icing that takes the hard work out of cake covering. Unopened, the Icing will keep satisfactorily for months as long as it is kept in a cool place.

As an alternative to elaborate Icing techniques, a multitude of attractive ingredients are available under the Topits range. Multi-coloured Sugar Strands, Hundreds and Thousands, Chocolate Chips, Jelly Diamonds and Orange and Lemon Slices are just some of the products that will bring fun and colour to cakes, ice cream and home-made desserts.

HINTS AND TIPS

Buttercream

To obtain best results, always use fresh butter at a temperature of 18-21°C (65-70°F) when making buttercream.

When colouring buttercream, add a few drops at a time as colourings can be strong and bitter.

Cakes and sponges

Many of the designs in this book are suitable for sponge or fruit cake.

A variety of shaped cake tins can be purchased or hired for a special occasion cake.

A shaped cake can also be made by pouring the batter into an ovenproof basin and baking in the usual way.

Coloured coconut

To colour coconut, add a few drops of edible food colouring and mix well.

Fixing

Use apricot purée when fixing cake to cake or almond paste to cake. Buttercream can be used to join sponge cakes.

Use cool boiled water or clear liquor when fixing sugarpaste to sugarpaste.

Use royal icing when fixing to royal icing.

Fix ribbons with either small dots or fine lines of royal icing.

Freezing

Sponges and swiss rolls can be batch baked and stored in a freezer for up to six months. Roll swiss rolls before freezing and store unfilled. Allow to thaw before unrolling and filling.

Grated chocolate

Chocolate can be coarsely grated with a cheese grater.

Melting compound or baker's chocolate

Slowly melt chocolate in a heat-proof bowl over hot water.

Use a small piping bag without a tube for fine piping or use plastic piping tubes for shells etc. Do not overfill the bag.

Keep the bag on a warm surface to avoid the chocolate setting in the bag.

White chocolate can be coloured with edible food colourings.

Piping gel

Clear piping gel is available from sugarcraft outlets and can be coloured with liquid or paste food colouring. Ready-made tubes of colour are available from supermarkets.

For piping, use a small piping bag without a tube. Do not overfill the bag.

Outline each section completely with royal icing or piping chocolate before filling with piping gel.

A little piping gel goes a very long way.

Piping Royal Icing

If necessary, practise piping on an upturned cake tin.

Always pipe on a dry surface.

Ensure that piped work is sufficiently dry to suport over-piping.

Portions

A 20.5cm (8") round sponge will provide approximately 16 portions. A 20.5cm (8") round fruit cake will provide approximately 40 portions and a square cake approximately 54 portions.

Royal Icing

Royal icing can be purchased ready-made if required.

Correctly prepared royal icing has a clean, glossy appearance, a good white colour and is light in texture.

When making royal icing add the icing sugar slowly to avoid a grainy texture before beating well.

Under mixed icing has a creamy look and should be beaten further.

Always make up sufficient coloured icing as it is virtually impossible to match the colour later.

Bowls of icing should be covered with a clean damp cloth to prevent drying out.

Royal icing can be stippled using a clean household sponge or a palette knife.

Soak used piping tubes overnight in cold water if royal icing has set inside them.

Sugarpaste

Sugarpaste can be purchased ready-made if required.

Sugarpaste should be made 24 hours before use. Store sugarpaste in a cool place (not a refrigerator) in an airtight container.

To colour sugarpaste, use edible food colouring. Dip a cocktail stick or skewer into the colour and add a very small amount at a time to the paste. Knead well until the colour is thoroughly mixed. Roll out paste thinly to check there is no streaking.

Mottled sugarpaste is made by half-kneading in the colour and then rolling out.

Always colour sufficient sugarpaste as it is virtually impossible to match the colour later.

Protect coloured sugarpaste from strong light.

Sugarpaste can be flavoured with a drop or two of flavouring to counteract sweetness.

If the paste is too dry, add a little white fat or egg white.

If the paste is too sticky, add a little cornflour or icing sugar.

Roll out sugarpaste on an icing sugar dusted surface.

In cold weather, warm the sugarpaste slightly in the oven.

The drying time for sugarpaste varies according to the weather and conditions in the kitchen. 24 hours is an approximate time.

Sugarpaste should be crimped or embossed before drying.

When crimping, hold the crimper at right angles to the cake and push gently into the paste before squeezing the crimper. Release the pressure and remove carefully.

To make frills, place the tapered end of a cocktail stick over the edge of thinly rolled sugarpaste and rock it back and forth covering a little at a time.

Timing

It is advisable to read through the selected design carefully before you start, checking what is required. Work backwards from the date the cake is needed and plan the timing. A fruit cake may need to mature, coatings to dry, or items to be purchased and time must be allowed for this.

A rich fruit cake takes approximately three weeks to mature.

ALL-IN-ONE SPONGE

This sponge is ideal for children's cakes or teatime treats as it is easy to make and has a light texture. It is, however, equally suitable for celebration cakes, particularly for the elderly who will appreciate its easily digestible quality.

RECIPE TABLES

SPONGE TIN SHAPES	SPONGE TIN SIZES					
ROUND	15cm (6")	18cm (7")	20.5cm (8")	23cm (9")	25.5cm (10")	28cm (11")
SQUARE	12.5cm (5")	15cm (6")	18cm (7")	20.5cm (8")	23cm (9")	25.5cm (10")
OVENPROOF BASIN	450ml (³/₄pt)	600ml (1pt)	750ml (1¼pt)	900ml (1½pt)	1 litre (1³/₄pt)	1200ml (2pt)
Self raising flour	60g (2oz)	85g (3oz)	115g (4oz)	170g (6oz)	225g (8oz)	285 (10oz)
Baking powder	½tsp	³/₄tsp	1tsp	1½tsp	2tsp	2½tsp
Soft (tub) margarine	60g (2oz)	85g (3oz)	115g (4oz)	170g (6oz)	225g (8oz)	285g (10oz)
Caster sugar	60g (2oz)	85g (3oz)	115g (4oz)	170g (6oz)	225g (8oz)	285g (10oz)
Fresh egg	60g (2oz)	85g (3oz)	115g (4oz)	170g (6oz)	225g (8oz)	285g (10oz)
Baking temperature	170°C (325°F) or Gas Mark 3					
Baking time (approximately)	20 mins	25 mins	30 mins	32 mins	35 mins	40 mins

NOTE: Baking time may need to be increased slightly for sponges baked in an ovenproof basin

BAKING TEST When the sponge has been baking for the recommended time, open the oven door slowly and, if sponge is pale in colour, continue baking. When the sponge is golden brown, draw fingers across the top (pressing lightly) and, if this action leaves an indentation, continue baking. Repeat test every 2-3 minutes until the top springs back when touched.

STORAGE The sponge may be wrapped in waxed paper and deep-frozen for up to 6 months. Use within 3 days of baking or after defrosting.

PORTIONS A 20.5cm (8") round sponge will provide approximately 16 portions.

CHOCOLATE SPONGE Replace 30g (1oz) of flour with 30g (1oz) of cocoa powder in the 20.5cm (8") round tin size recipe and pro rata for the other recipes.

1

Grease tins with butter and line the bases with greased greaseproof paper.

2

Place all the ingredients together in a mixing bowl.

3

Beat the ingredients together for 3-4 minutes, until thoroughly mixed and of a light consistency.

4

Divide the mixture evenly between the prepared tins. Bake in the pre-heated oven for recommended baking time. Test before removing – see page 12.

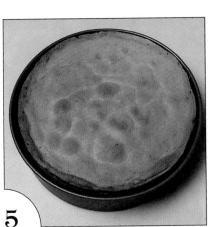

5

After baking, leave the sponges in the tins for 5 minutes before turning out onto a wire cooling tray.

ALL-IN-ONE SWISS ROLL

Swiss Rolls are easy to make and form a useful and versatile base for a cake. They can be filled with a variety of fillings and then coated in buttercream or cream, flavoured and coloured if required. Swiss Rolls can also be covered in sugarpaste over a layer of butttercream.

SPONGE TIN SIZE 18 x 28cm (7 x 11")

Soft (tub) margarine	60g (2oz)	
Caster sugar	115g (4oz)	Filling of choice
Fresh egg	115g (4oz)	Caster sugar for dusting
Self raising flour	115g (4oz)	

Baking temperature 200°C (400°F) or Gas Mark 6

BAKING TEST When the sponge has been baking for the recommended time, open the oven door slowly and, if sponge is pale in colour, continue baking. When the sponge is golden brown, draw fingers across the top (pressing lightly) and, if this action leaves an indentation, continue baking. Repeat test every 1-2 minutes until the top springs back when touched.

STORAGE The filled sponge may be wrapped in waxed paper and deep-frozen for up to 6 months. Use within 3 days of baking or after defrosting.

1

Lightly grease a swiss roll tin 18 x 28cm (7 x 11") with margarine. Line the tin with greaseproof paper then grease the paper.

2

Place all the ingredients into a mixing bowl.

3

Beat together until light, white and creamy.

4

Using a spatula, spread the mixture evenly in the tin.

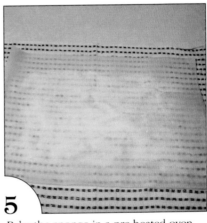

5

Bake the sponge in a pre-heated oven for 10-12 minutes. Whilst the sponge is baking, place greaseproof paper onto a tea towel and sprinkle with caster sugar.

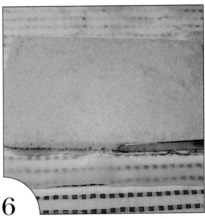

6

When baked, immediately turn the sponge out onto the sugared paper. Carefully remove the lining paper. Then trim the crust from the sponge-sides.

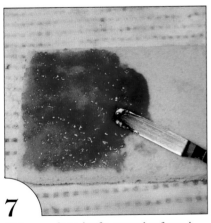

7

Using a palette knife, spread softened jam evenly over the sponge.

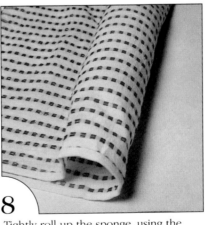

8

Tightly roll up the sponge, using the towel to keep the pressure even.

9

When cool, remove the towel and place the swiss roll onto a wire tray to cool completely. Remove the outer crust with a knife before coating with cream.

ALL-IN-ONE FRUIT CAKE

RECIPE TABLES

CAKE TIN SHAPES	CAKE TIN SIZES					
ROUND	15cm (6")	18cm (7")	20.5cm (8")	23cm (9")	25.5cm (10")	28cm (11")
SQUARE	12.5cm (5")	15cm (6")	18cm (7")	20.5cm (8")	23cm (9")	25.5cm (10")
Self raising flour	100g (3½oz)	145g (5oz)	200g (7oz)	225g (8oz)	315g (11oz)	400g (14oz)
Ground nutmeg	pinch	¼tsp	½tsp	½tsp	¾tsp	1tsp
Ground mixed spice	¼tsp	½tsp	½tsp	¾tsp	1tsp	1½tsp
Ground mace	small pinch	small pinch	medium pinch	medium pinch	large pinch	large pinch
Sultanas	85g (3oz)	130g (4½oz)	170g (6oz)	215g (7½oz)	285g (10oz)	340g (12oz)
Currants	85g (3oz)	130g (4½oz)	170g (6oz)	215g (7½oz)	285g (10oz)	340g (12oz)
Raisins	85g (3oz)	130g (4½oz)	170g (6oz)	215g (7½oz)	285g (10oz)	340g (12oz)
Glacé cherries	45g (1½oz)	65g (2¼oz)	85g (3oz)	105g (3¾oz)	145g (5oz)	170g (6oz)
Mixed peel	45g (1½oz)	65g (2¼oz)	85g (3oz)	105g (3¾oz)	145g (5oz)	170g (6oz)
Lemon zest (lemons)	¼	½	½	1	1½	2
Ground almonds	22g (¾oz)	30g (1oz)	45g (1½oz)	50g (1¾oz)	75g (2½oz)	85g (3oz)
Soft (tub) margarine	85g (3oz)	130g (4½oz)	170g (6oz)	215g (7½oz)	285g (10oz)	340g (12oz)
Soft light brown sugar	85g (3oz)	130g (4½oz)	170g (6oz)	215g (7½oz)	285g (10oz)	340g (12oz)
Fresh egg	85g (3oz)	130g (4½oz)	170g (6oz)	215g (7½oz)	285g (10oz)	340g (12oz)
Rum	½tbls	½tbls	1tbls	1tbls	1½tbls	2tbls
Black treacle	1tbls	1tbls	1½tbls	1½tbls	2tbls	3tbls
Baking temperature	150℃ (300°F) or Gas Mark 2			140℃ (275°F) or Gas Mark 1		
Baking time (approximately)	1½ hrs	1¾ hrs	2 hrs	2½ hrs	3 hrs	3½ hrs

BAKING TEST At the end of the recommended baking time, bring the cake forward from the oven so that it can be tested. Then insert a stainless steel skewer into the centre of the cake and slowly withdraw it. The skewer should be as clean as it went in. This means the cake is sufficiently baked. If cake mixture clings to the skewer, remove the skewer completely and continue baking at the same temperature. Test thereafter every 10 minutes until the skewer is clean when withdrawn from the cake.

STORAGE When the cake is cold carefully remove from the tin, then remove the greaseproof paper. Wrap the cake in waxed paper and leave in a cupboard for three weeks to mature.

PORTIONS To calculate the estimated number of portions that can be cut from the finished cake, firstly add together the total weight of the cake ingredients, almond paste, sugarpaste or/and royal icing to be used. An average cut piece of finished cake weighs 60g (2oz) therefore divide accordingly.

Approximate portions:

Round cakes	Portions	Square cakes	Portions
13cm (5")	14	13cm (5")	16
15cm (6")	22	15cm (6")	27
18cm (7")	30	18cm (7")	40
20.5cm (8")	40	20.5cm (8")	54
23cm (9")	54	23cm (9")	70
25.5cm (10")	68	25.5cm (10")	90
30cm (12")	100	30cm (12")	134

Tiered cakes	Round cakes	Square cakes
2-tier 18 & 25.5cm (7 & 10")	98	130
3-tier 15, 20.5, 25.5cm (6, 8, 10")	130	171
3-tier 13, 18, 23cm (5, 7, 9")	98	126

Fruit cake makes an ideal base for both sugarpaste and royal iced celebration cakes, and it is the traditional medium for wedding cakes as it has excellent keeping properties. Timing is important when making a fruit cake, as it needs at least three weeks to mature before use.

INGREDIENTS for 20.5cm (8") round or 18cm (7") square cake.

Self-raising flour	200g (7oz)
Ground nutmeg	½ teaspoon
Ground mixed spice	½ teaspoon
Ground mace	medium pinch
Sultanas	170g (6oz)
Currants	170g (6oz)
Raisins	170g (6oz)
Glacé cherries	85g (3oz)
Mixed peel	85g (3oz)
Lemon	zest of ½
Ground almonds	45g (1½oz)
Soft (tub) margarine	170g (6oz)
Soft light brown sugar	170g (6oz)
Fresh egg	170g (6oz)
Rum	1 tablespoon
Black treacle	1½ tablespoons

ITEMS REQUIRED

Round cake tin 20.5cm (8")
x 7.5cm (3") deep
Greaseproof paper and margarine
Wire cooling tray

Bake at 150°C (300°F) or Gas Mark 2 for approximately 2 hours.

BAKING TEST see page 16

STORAGE see page 16

See page 16 for ingredients of other cake tin sizes.

1 Cut greaseproof paper 5cm (2") deeper than the cake-tin to cover inside. Cut along bottom edge 2.5cm (1") up at intervals. Cut a circle for the base.

2 Brush the inside of cake tin with soft margarine.

3 Cover the side with the greaseproof paper then place the circle into the bottom. Brush the greaseproof paper with margarine.

4 Carefully weigh all the ingredients separately. Chop the cherries in half. Clean and then remove any stalks from the fruit.

5 Grate the lemon. Mix fruit together with the rum in a bowl. Leave all ingredients overnight in a warm place 18°C (65°F).

6 Sieve the flour, nutmeg, spice and mace together three times.

7 Place all the ingredients, except the fruit, into a mixing bowl.

8 Beat together for approximately 2 minutes on high speed to form a batter.

9 Stir in the fruit, using a large spoon, until all the fruit is mixed into the batter.

10 Spread mixture into prepared cake tin. Place tray of hot water at bottom of pre-heated oven. Then place cake in centre of oven.

11 Remove water halfway through baking time. Continue baking. If necessary cover the cake-top with paper. Test after recommended baking time – see page 16.

12 When baked remove cake from oven and leave in the tin on a wire tray for 24 hours. See page 16 for storage instructions.

ALMOND PASTE

Almond paste differs from marzipan in that almond paste is a mixture of uncooked ground almonds, sugar and glucose or eggs, whereas marzipan is made from cooked ground almonds and sugar. Either paste is suitable for covering cakes. Almond paste can be stored in food-approved polythene or in a sealed container in a cool, dry place. Do not overmix the paste and never allow almond paste to come into contact with flour.

INGREDIENTS (recipe 1)		INGREDIENTS (recipe 2)	
Icing sugar	170g (6oz)	Icing sugar	225g (8oz)
Caster sugar	170g (6oz)	Caster sugar	225g (8oz)
Ground almonds	340g (12oz)	Ground almonds	445g (16oz)
Glucose syrup	225g (8oz)	Egg yolks	approximately 6

1
Carefully sieve the icing sugar twice.

2
Place the dry ingredients into a mixing bowl and stir together using a hook shaped beater.

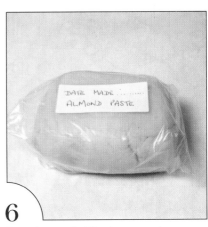

3
For recipe 1, warm the glucose syrup in a separate bowl in hot water.

4
Pour the warmed glucose syrup, or egg yolks, into the dry ingredients.

5
Mix all the ingredients together until a pliable paste is formed. Add more glucose syrup, or egg yolks, if necessary.

6
Store in a sealed food-approved polythene bag, with the date it was made, until required.

BUTTERCREAM

Buttercream is an ideal medium for coating children's cakes as it is easily coloured and flavoured. To vary the taste and texture of buttercream beat in any of the following: whisked egg white, milk, egg, marshmallow, fondant, condensed milk, and edible colours and flavourings. To obtain the best results, always use fresh butter at a temperature of 18-21°C (65-70°F).

INGREDIENTS

Butter	115g (4oz)
Icing sugar	170-225g (6-8oz)
Warm water	1-2 tablespoons
Food colouring	
Flavouring	

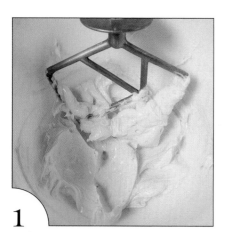

1
Soften the butter and beat until it is light and fluffy.

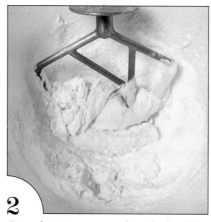

2
Sieve the icing sugar and gradually add to the butter, beating well after each addition.

3
Add the warm water, and flavouring. Beat the mixture once again.

4
Strained fruit juice of choice can be used as a flavouring if desired.

5
Add and thoroughly mix in the appropriate food colouring if required.

6
For chocolate flavoured buttercream quickly stir in melted chocolate. Use 60g (2oz) of chocolate to 225g (8oz) of buttercream.

ALBUMEN SOLUTION

When making albumen solution it is essential that all utensils are sterilised and free from grease. When the albumen powder is mixed into the water, it will go lumpy. After 1 hour, stirring occasionally, the lumps will dissolve to form a smooth liquid. Once the solution has been made, it should be kept in a refrigerator in a sealed container. Bring to room temperature before use.

INGREDIENTS

Pure albumen powder	15g (½oz)
Water	85g (3oz)

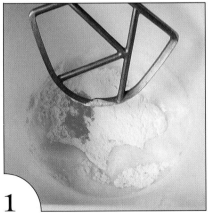

1
Pour the water into a bowl and stir whilst sprinkling in the powdered albumen.

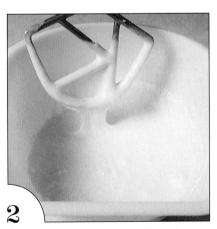

2
Thoroughly mix with the whisk, but do not beat. Leave for 1 hour, stirring occasionally.

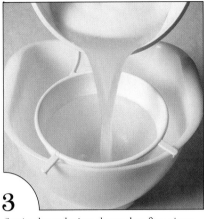

3
Strain the solution through a fine sieve or muslin. It is then ready for use.

ROYAL ICING

INGREDIENTS

Fresh egg white or	
albumen solution	100g (3½oz)
Sieved icing sugar	455g (16oz)

Note: If using fresh egg whites separate 24 hours before required.

GLYCERIN – Table for use

For soft cutting royal icing add to every 455g (1lb) of prepared royal icing:
1 teaspoon of glycerin for the bottom tier of a three-tier cake.
2 teaspoons of glycerin for middle tier of a three-tier cake.
3 teaspoons of glycerin for top tier or for single-tier cakes.

1
Pour the fresh egg whites or albumen solution into a mixing bowl. Stir in half the sieved icing sugar until dissolved.

2
Stir in remaining sugar and then clean down the inside of the bowl.

3
Beat mixture until light and fluffy and peaks can be formed. Scrape down inside of bowl and cover with a damp cloth.

SUGARPASTE

Sugarpaste is ideal for covering cakes. It is also easily shaped with the fingers for modelling animals, figures and flowers. Colourings and flavourings can be kneaded into the paste, but care should be taken that sufficient quantity is coloured to complete each project. Fix sugarpaste to sugarpaste with pure alcohol, such as vodka or gin; egg white, royal icing or cooled boiled water.

INGREDIENTS

Water	2 tablespoons
Powdered gelatine	1½ level teaspoons
Liquid glucose	1½ tablespoons
Glycerin	2 teaspoons
Sieved icing sugar	455g (16oz)

Storage: Sugarpaste should be kept in a food-approved polythene bag in a refrigerator. It will keep for up to 2 weeks. The bag should be clearly labelled with the date it was made. Bring to room temperature before use.

MODELLING PASTE: add 2 teaspoons of gum tragacanth to the basic sugarpaste recipe and work well in. Leave for 24 hours before use. Store as for sugarpaste.

1 Pour the water into a stainless steel or non-stick saucepan. Sprinkle on the powdered gelatine and dissolve over a low heat.

2 Add the glucose and glycerin and stir in before removing the saucepan from the heat.

3 Add the icing sugar gradually, mixing continuously with a spoon to avoid any lumps developing.

4 Continue adding the icing sugar until it is no longer possible to stir the mixture.

5 Remove the spoon and add the remaining icing sugar by kneading the mixture between fingers and thumb.

6 Continue kneading the paste until clear and smooth. The paste is then ready for use. See above for storage.

COVERING A FRUIT CAKE WITH SUGARPASTE OR CAKE COVERING

1

Fill in the cake-top imperfections with small pieces of almond paste and then brush boiled apricot purée over the whole cake-top and side.

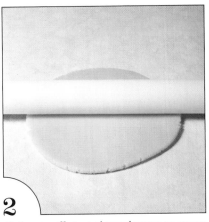

2

Roll out sufficient almond paste to cover the entire cake.

3

Place the almond paste over the rolling pin and slowly unroll it onto the cake, as shown.

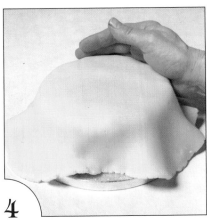

4

Lightly press and smooth the almond paste against the cake surface to expel any trapped air.

5

Trim the surplus almond paste from the cake-base, keeping the knife tight against the cake-side. Leave to dry for 24 hours.

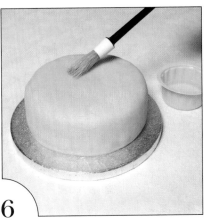

6

Brush clear alcohol (e.g. gin or vodka) over the almond paste.

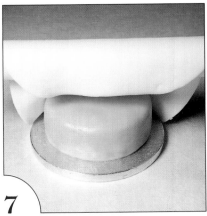

7

Immediately roll out sufficient sugarpaste (made 24 hours before use) and place over the cake, using the rolling pin as shown.

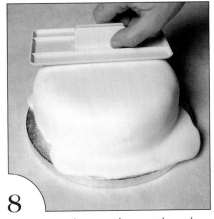

8

Rotating a cake smoother, gently push the sugarpaste onto the cake to flatten the surface.

9

Trim the surplus sugarpaste from the cake-base keeping the knife tight against the cake-side.

COVERING A CAKE-TOP WITH ALMOND PASTE

Almond paste or ready-made marzipan can be used to cover a cake. Always ensure that the layer is thick enough to prevent the cake from discolouring the icing.

It is important to prepare the cake properly before covering by removing the top of a dome-shaped cake or filling in any imperfections with almond paste. Ensure that the sides are straight and properly square. Any burnt fruit should be removed.

Almond paste should be rolled out on an icing or caster sugar dusted surface. Never use flour or cornflour as this could cause fermentation.

Apricot purée is the most suitable fixing agent as it has least colour and flavour. This should be boiled before use and brushed on immediately.

The covered cake should be left to stand in a dry room 18°C (65°F) for 24 hours before decorating. Never store a covered cake in a sealed plastic container.

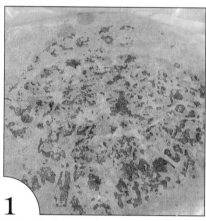

1
It is advisable to use a cake which has matured (the outside of the cake is then moist). This usually takes two to three weeks after the cake has been made.

2
Remove the waxed paper, place the cake upside down onto a board and brush brandy or rum over the surface (1 teaspoon per 455g (1lb) of cake).

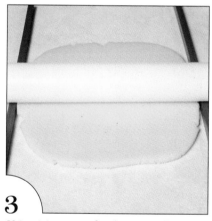

3
Using icing sugar for dusting, roll out almond paste between spacers to achieve an even thickness.

4
Cut the almond paste into a disc the same size as the cake-top using a cake tin base or template as guide.

5
Thinly spread boiled apricot purée over the almond paste, then upturn the cake onto the almond paste, as shown.

6
Upturn the cake and place onto a cake card or board. Wrap side in waxed paper. Leave to dry for 24 hours before decorating.

COVERING A CAKE WITH ALMOND PASTE

1

Round cake: Almond paste the cake-top (see p.24). Roll out, onto icing sugar, one piece of almond paste three times the diameter of the cake.

2

Cut the strip of almond paste to approximately the depth of the cake.

3

Spread boiled apricot purée over the strip of almond paste.

4

Fix the almond paste to the cake side, using flat of the hand and cut to correct length.

5

Trim the surplus from the cake-top edge, keeping the knife close to the surface. Leave to dry 3 days before coating with royal icing.

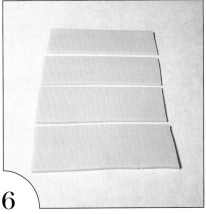

6

Square cake: Almond paste the cake-top (see p.24). Roll out and cut four strips of almond paste, the same size as the cake side.

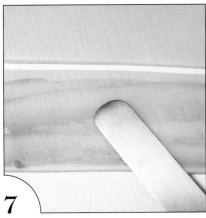

7

Spread boiled apricot purée over each strip.

8

Press each strip firmly to the cake sides, as shown.

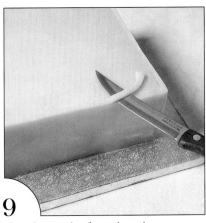

9

Trim the surplus from the cake-top edge, keeping the knife close to the surface. Leave to dry 3 days before coating with royal icing.

COATING CAKES WITH ROYAL ICING

Royal icing is the traditional medium for coating celebration cakes and its beautiful, smooth finish is perfect for formal piped designs. Ready-to-mix and ready-made royal icings are now available which are ideal for the absolute beginner to work with as they are extremely easy to apply and ensure a good result.

Getting as good a shape as possible at the almond paste stage will make coating easier. Always ensure that the top is flat and the sides vertical as this enables a smooth layer of icing to be laid down. The almond paste covered cake should be left for at least 24 hours before coating.

To produce a good finish, it is essential that care should be taken when making the icing, and when coating, as the slightest lump will mar the smoothness. All items used in preparation, coating and decorating should be scrupulously clean.

Icing for coating should be made 24 hours in advance and stirred immediately before use to disperse any bubbles. The consistency should form soft peaks and a drop of water can be added if the icing is too stiff to spread easily. A very small amount of blue colour can be added to improve the whiteness but blue should not be added to icing which will be coloured further. A table for the addition of glycerin to produce soft-cutting royal icing is on page 21.

The icing should be stored in a closed container and a small amount transferred to a separate bowl, covered with a damp cloth. The icing should be kept well scraped down to prevent drying out.

A stiff, stainless steel palette knife is ideal for spreading the royal icing and a stainless steel ruler can be used for flattening and levelling the top surface. When using side scrapers, the fingers should be spread across the width of the scraper to ensure an even pressure when rotating the turntable. It is preferable for the cake to have at least three thin coats, each coat being allowed to dry before applying the next. When using coloured icing, the first coat should be white, the second a pale shade of the colour required, and the third coat the actual colour. Coloured icing will dry patchy unless evenly applied.

When the covering is complete, the cake should be left to stand overnight in a warm room 18°C (65°F) before decorating. Do not store a coated cake in a sealed plastic container.

As royal icing is a form of meringue, it must be well beaten as otherwise the icing is heavy and difficult to handle. Under-mixed icing has a slightly creamy look and should be beaten further. Over-beating the icing, in a high speed mixer for instance, incorporates too much air and causes the icing to become fluffy. If the icing sugar is added too quickly, then the icing becomes grainy in appearance. Correctly made royal icing has a clean, white colour and is slightly glossy and light in texture.

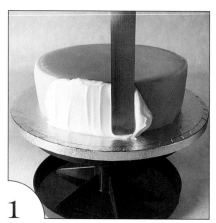

1
To coat a round cake: Place the cake with board onto a turntable. Using a palette knife, spread royal icing around the cake side.

2
To smooth, hold a scraper against the cake-side and rotate the turntable one complete turn. Repeat until smooth.

3
Remove the surplus royal icing from the cake-top and board, using a palette knife. Leave to dry for 12 hours.

4 Spread royal icing evenly over the cake-top using a paddling movement with a palette knife.

5 Level the icing using a stainless steel rule in a backwards and forwards motion over the cake-top until smooth.

6 Remove the surplus icing from the edge of the cake-top and leave to dry for 12 hours. Repeat steps 1-6 for two more layers.

7 **To coat straight sided cakes:** Coat opposite sides with royal icing, remove surplus and leave to dry for 12 hours. Repeat until all sides are covered.

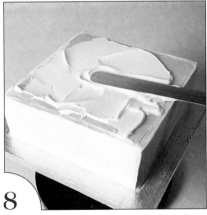

8 Spread royal icing evenly over the cake-top using a paddling movement with the palette knife.

9 Level the icing using a stainless steel rule in a backwards and forwards motion over the cake-top until smooth.

10 Remove the surplus royal icing from the edges of the cake. Leave to dry for 12 hours. Repeat steps 7-10 for two more layers.

11 **To coat a cake board:** Using a palette knife, spread royal icing over the cake board surface, as shown.

12 Smooth the royal icing, holding the scraper steady while rotating the turntable. Clean sides. Leave to dry for 12 hours then decorate as required.

LAYERING AND COATING A SPONGE

1
Remove the top crust from two sponges. Upturn and remove the bottom crust.

2
Place one sponge on a cake board and cover the top with jam or preserve. Place second sponge on top.

3
Place on a turntable. Cover the sponge-top with buttercream, rotate the turntable as you work, and smooth with a palette knife.

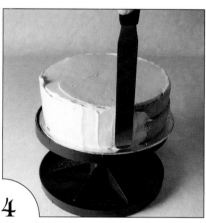

4
Spread buttercream around the side of the sponge with a palette knife.

5
Smooth the side whilst rotating turntable. Remove surplus buttercream from the top-edge. Place in a refrigerator for 1 hour and coat again if required.

6
Alternative coating patterns
Apply a second coat of buttercream to cake top. Draw a serrated scraper across one half of the top in a zigzag motion.

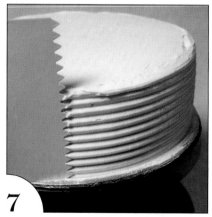

7
Apply a second coat of buttercream to the cake-side and hold a serrated scraper firmly against the side. Rotate the turntable.

8
Coat the cake-side with buttercream. Move the scraper in waves, whilst turning the turntable, to produce a zigzag effect.

9
Coat the cake-side with buttercream. Hold the coated cake in palm of hand. Fill other hand with roasted nibbed almonds and palm onto cake-side until evenly covered.

FRILLS AND CRIMPING

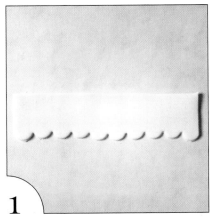

1 Cut the shape shown from rolled out sugarpaste.

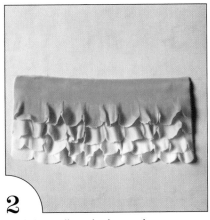

2 Frill the scalloped edge as shown. Repeat as required. Moisten the straight edges and fix the layers, as shown.

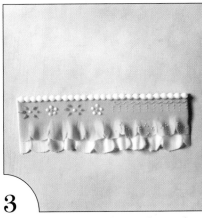

3 Decorate the frills by piping dots and small shells, as shown, using royal icing.

4 Lightly dust the work surface with a little cornflour and roll out sugarpaste. Cut the shape shown.

5 Place the tapered end of a cocktail stick over the edge of the circle and rock it back and forth to create a frill.

6 Cut the frilled circle in half. Moisten with a little water and fix to the cake, as required.

1 A crimping tool of appropriate shape is required. Place a rubber band around the tool to bring the teeth 6mm (¼") apart.

2 Dip the teeth into sieved icing sugar and tap off the surplus.

3 Push the teeth into newly rolled sugarpaste, squeeze together then gently release and raise the crimper. Repeat at even thickness the shape required.

MAKING A PIPING BAG

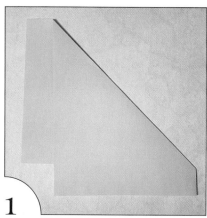

1
Size of greaseproof required: Large bags 45.5 x 35.5cm (18 x 14"); Medium 35.5 x 25.5cm (14 x 10"); Small 25.5 x 20.5cm (10 x 8"). Fold as shown.

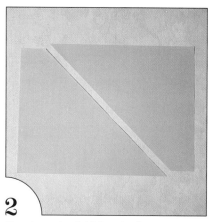

2
Cut along the fold line (to form two identical shapes).

3
Turn one piece of greaseproof paper long edge uppermost. Pick up the top right hand corner and start to turn it towards the centre, form a cone.

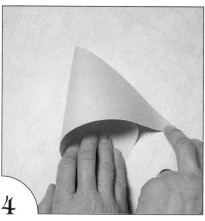

4
With the other hand, lift the opposite corner completely over the cone.

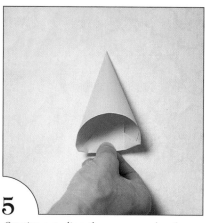

5
Continue curling the paper under the cone and pull taut, until a sharp point is formed at the tip.

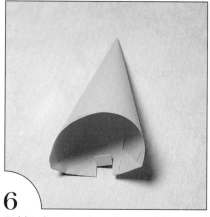

6
Fold in loose ends and cut and fold the small section shown to secure the bag.

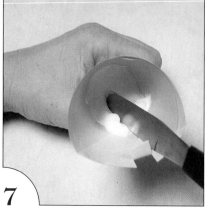

7
Cut tip off bag to hold a piping tube. Drop tube in and, using a palette knife, half fill the bag with royal icing or buttercream.

8
Flatten the wide part of the bag and gently squeeze filling down to the tube. Fold each side of the bag to the centre.

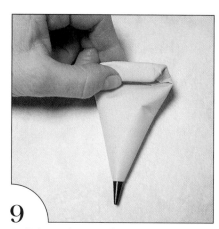

9
Roll the wide end of the bag towards the tube to seal the bag. It is then ready for use.

MAKING TEMPLATES

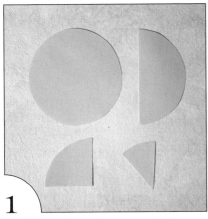

1

Petal template: Cut a paper circle to the same size as the cake-top. Fold in half, then half again and in half once more.

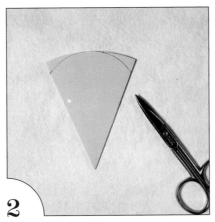

2

Mark the paper as shown and, using sharp scissors, carefully cut along the line whilst keeping the paper folded.

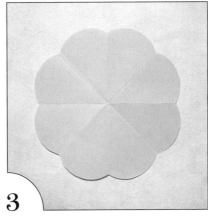

3

Unfold the template and check with the picture that it is correct. Place between two flat surfaces to flatten out.

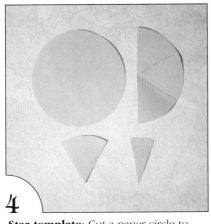

4

Star template: Cut a paper circle to the same size as the cake-top. Fold in half, then into three and finally in half again.

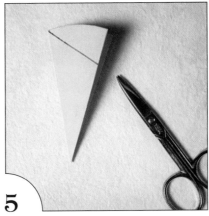

5

Mark the paper as shown and, using sharp scissors, carefully cut along the line whilst keeping the paper folded.

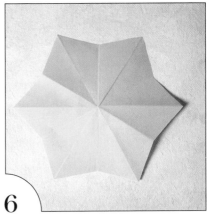

6

Unfold the template and check with the picture that it is correct. Place between two flat surfaces to flatten out.

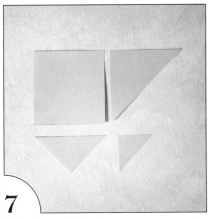

7

Floral template: Cut a paper square to the same size as the cake-top. Fold diagonally, then in half and in half again.

8

Mark the paper as shown and, using sharp scissors, carefully cut along the line whilst keeping the paper folded.

9

Unfold the template and check with the picture that it is correct. Place between two flat surfaces to flatten out.

PIPED SHAPES

1

Star: Hold piping bag still in a vertical position and press. At required size, stop pressing and lift bag upright.

2

Rosette: Press upright piping bag whilst turning in a clockwise motion. On completion of one turn stop pressing and draw bag away.

3

'C' line: Pipe in anti-clockwise and upward direction. Form tail, stop pressing and slide tube on surface.

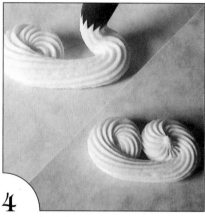

4

Lateral 'C' line: Pipe in anti-clockwise direction for first curve. Continue piping to form the matching curve. Stop pressing, lift bag upright.

5

Skein: Pipe an anti-clockwise curve. Continue in clockwise direction to form matching curve. Stop pressing and lift bag upright.

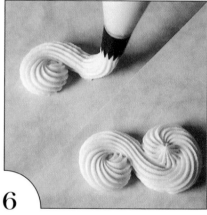

6

Reversed skein: Pipe a clockwise curve. Continue in anti-clockwise direction to form matching curve. Stop pressing and lift bag upright.

7

Shell: Hold piping bag at angle shown. Press to the required size. Stop pressing, then slide piping tube down along surface to form tail.

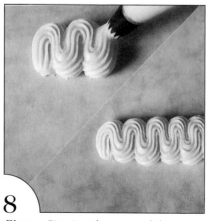

8

Zigzag: Pipe in tight waves whilst keeping piping tube on the surface. Continue piping an even zigzag. Stop pressing and slide piping tube away.

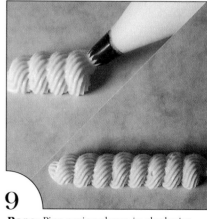

9

Rope: Pipe spring-shape in clockwise direction, using even pressure and keeping bag horizontal. Stop pressing and pull bag away in a half-turn.

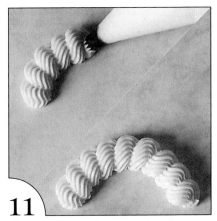

10

Convex rope: Pipe curved spring-shape in clockwise direction, using even pressure, keeping bag horizontal. Stop pressing, pull away in a half-turn.

11

Concave rope: Pipe curved spring-shape in clockwise direction, using even pressure, keeping bag horizontal. Stop pressing, pull away in a half-turn.

12

Spiral shell: Pipe in clockwise direction, increasing the size of each circle then decreasing. Stop pressing, pull away in a half-turn.

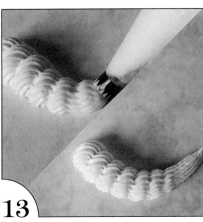

13

'C' scroll: Pipe in clockwise direction, increasing then decreasing each circle size, to form tail. Stop pressing and slide away.

14

Reversed 'C' scroll: Pipe in clockwise direction, increasing then decreasing each circle size, to form tail. Stop pressing and slide away.

15

'S' scroll: Hold piping bag at angle shown and start to press in clockwise direction, increasing the size of each circle to form body.

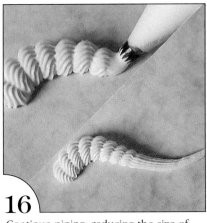

16

Continue piping, reducing the size of the circles from the centre. Then form the tail by reducing pressure during piping. Stop pressing and slide away.

17

Reversed 'S' scroll: Hold piping bag at angle shown and start to press in an anti-clockwise direction, increasing the size of each circle to form body.

18

Continue piping, reducing the size of the circles from the centre. Then form the tail by reducing pressure during piping. Stop pressing and slide away.

LEIGH

1 Cover a petal shaped cake and board with sugarpaste. Then pipe shells (No.43) with royal icing around the cake-base.

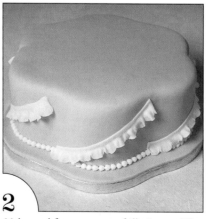

2 Make and fix sugarpaste frills (see p.29) to the cake-side as shown.

3 Pipe shells along the top edge of each frill (No.43).

4
Pipe lines and leaf shapes as shown (No.1) around the cake-top edge.

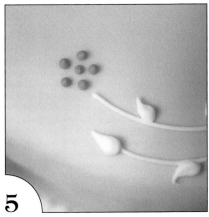

5
Pipe a series of dots (No.1) to resemble flower heads.

6
Cut out and frill the edge of two appropriate sized sugarpaste discs.

7
Fix the discs together and decorate with piped dots (No.1). Then fix cherub or baby on top.

8
Fix the disc onto the cake-top and decorate with ribbon, bows and dove.

9
Pipe recipient's name in the style shown (No.1).

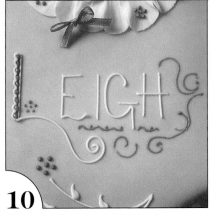

10
Decorate the name with piped tracery and dots (No.1).

11
Pipe leaves and dots (No.1) over base of cake-side frill.

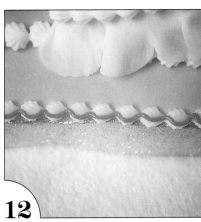

12
Pipe shells around the board edge (No.42) then pipe a line over the shells (No.1).

RODDY

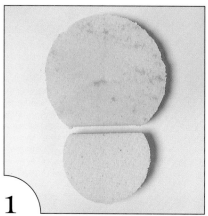

1 Cut two round sponges (one larger than the other) to shape them.

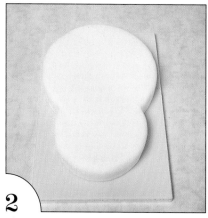

2 Place together and cover with sugarpaste. Then place onto a sugarpaste covered board.

3 Pipe shells around the base with royal icing (containing glycerin) or buttercream (No.7).

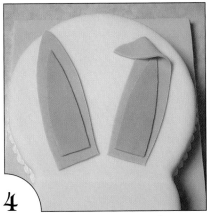

4 Cut out sugarpaste ear pieces, fix together before fixing and folding onto the sponge top, as shown.

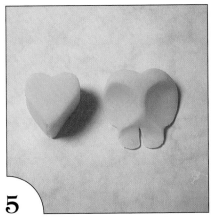

5 Cut out thick sugarpaste with a heart-shaped cutter. Press both sides down with thumbs, then press front and cut to form nose and teeth.

6 Fix in position. Then cut and fix eyes. Pipe the whiskers shown (No.1).

TEMPLATES

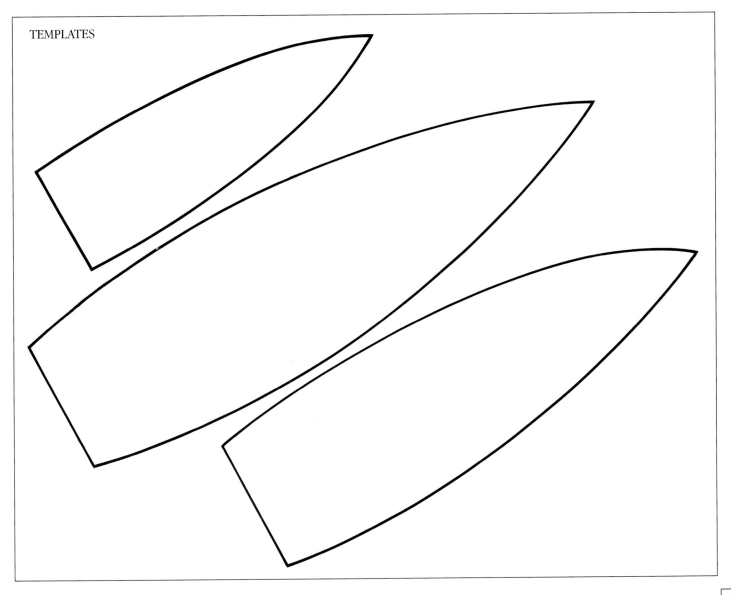

THEO

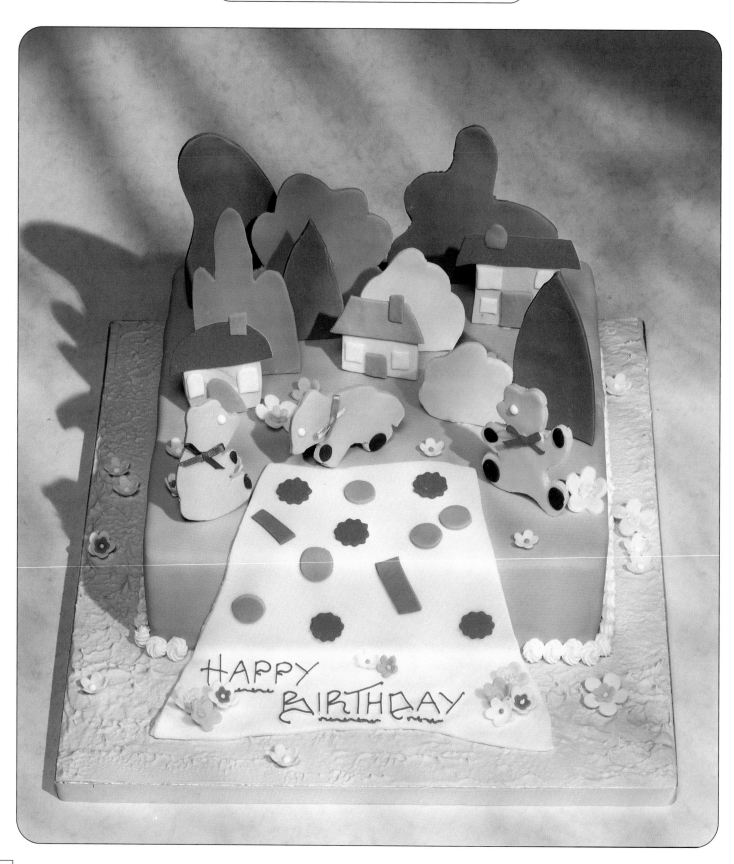

HAPPY BIRTHDAY

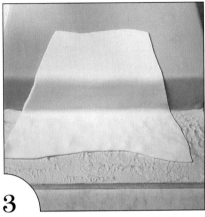

1 Cover the cake with sugarpaste, placed on the cake board as shown. Stipple the board with royal icing.

2 Using the templates as a guide, cut out shapes required from modelling paste (see p.22). Decorate, then leave to dry.

3 Cut out and fix a sugarpaste tablecloth over the cake-top and down onto the board.

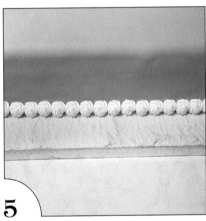

4 Cut out and fix sugarpaste shapes and flowers as required. Pipe inscription of choice (No.1)

5 Pipe rosettes around the cake-base, excluding the tablecloth (No.7).

6 Fix the teddy bears into position with royal icing.

7 Fix the houses as shown.

8 Carefully fix the bushes and trees.

9 Cut out and fix further flowers, as required, onto the cake-top and board.

TEMPLATES

HARDY

1 Cover a cake with mottled sugarpaste (see p.11). Then stipple royal icing around the cake board.

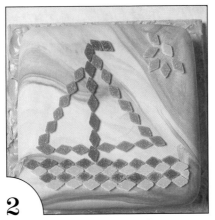

2 Fix jelly diamonds, with royal icing, to make an appropriate picture on the cake-top.

3 Follow the theme around the cake-sides with further jelly diamonds. Then pipe royal icing dots (No.1) as shown.

RYAN

1

Cover an elongated octagonal-shaped sponge with sugarpaste. Then spread royal icing over remaining cake board surface. Leave to dry for 24 hours.

2

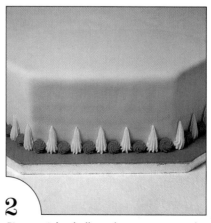

Pipe upright shells and rosettes around the cake-base, using royal icing (No.7).

3

Cut out a figure 2 from sugarpaste and fix to the cake-top. Pipe message of choice (No.2). Overpipe the No.2 line (No.1).

4 Using the templates as a guide (see index), pipe the soldiers, as shown (No.1). Leave to dry for 1 hour.

5 Fill-in each section with piping gel using various colours (see p.11).

6 Pipe bulbs on each side of the cake-top edge as shown (No.2). Pipe the ground, then a line beside the bulbs (No.1). Fix ribbon around the cake board edge.

TEMPLATE

OLLIE

1
Place a small piece of sponge onto the main sponge top and cover all over with buttercream.

2
Cover with sugarpaste. Cut out and fix sugarpaste eyes. Then dab colouring, using a sponge-stick (see index) to create the pupils.

3
Cut out and fix sugarpaste nose, mouth, eyebrows and ears (fold as shown). Then fix ribbon around the base.

44

TEMPLATE

RUPERT

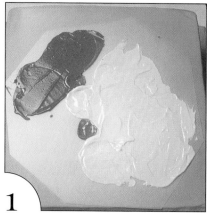

1 Coat a cake with royal icing. Leave to dry for 24 hours. Place stencil on cake (see index). Spread softened royal icing over the stencil as shown.

2 Scrape the surplus icing off the stencil with a palette knife held flat. Then carefully lift the stencil away in one continuous movement.

3 Repeat steps 1 and 2 around the cake-sides. Place sitting teddy bear in centre and teddy bear with balloons at corners (reverse stencil as shown).

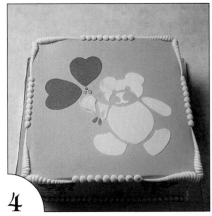

4 Pipe scrolls and shells with royal icing (No.43) around the cake-top edge and base.

5 Pipe grass in the places shown (No.1).

6 Pipe inscription of choice (No.2). Decorate the cake with flowers and bows. Then pipe graduated dots and tracery (No.1).

TEMPLATES

SPOT

1 Place two mounds of sugarpaste (to form cheeks) onto a buttercream coated sponge.

2 Cover with sugarpaste. Using a sponge-stick (see index) dab colouring onto the surface for large spots.

3 Using a dowel, dipped in colouring, dab spots onto the cheeks as shown. Pipe lines (No.1) to form the mouth.

4 Cut out and fix sugarpaste eyes and tongue. Roll a piece of sugarpaste into nose shape and fix.

5 Cut out the ears. Then cut out and fix an inner ear. Fix both ears in position, folding as shown.

6 Make and fix ribbon around the base in design shown.

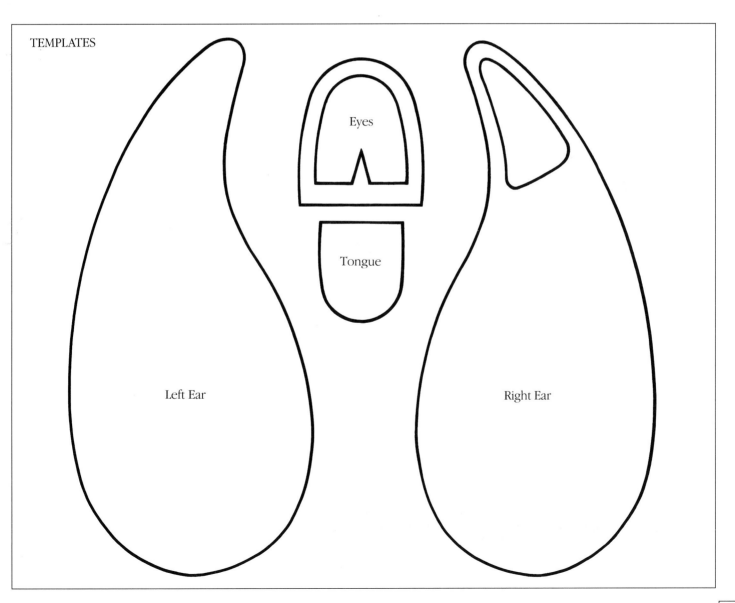

TEMPLATES

Eyes

Tongue

Left Ear

Right Ear

BUNNIE

1

Using the template as a guide, cut out and fix sugarpaste pieces onto a sugarpaste covered sponge to form mummy rabbit.

2

Cut out and fix sugarpaste pieces of baby rabbit to the cake-top.

3

Decorate the mummy rabbit with royal icing (No.1).

4 Decorate the baby rabbit with royal icing (No.1).

5 Pipe rabbits around the cake-base (No.2) and pipe grass as shown (No.1).

6 Pipe inscription of choice (No.2) then pipe tracery (No.1) and grass below rabbits. Fix flowers to the rabbits and fix candles as required.

TEMPLATES

PERRY

1 Cut two round sponges (one larger than the other) to shape shown. Place on an oval board and cover with sugarpaste.

2 Using the template as a guide, cut out and fix sugarpaste pieces shown.

3 Cut out and fix further sugarpaste pieces, then using a sponge-stick (see index) dab food colouring onto the eyes for pupils.

TEMPLATE

SETH

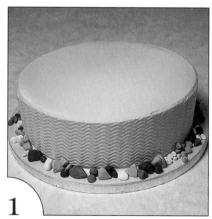

1
Coat a sponge with royal icing, using a comb scraper to create wave effect around the sponge-side. Make and fix sugarpaste rocks around the board.

2
Using the template as a guide, pipe the boat, mast and sail with melted chocolate (see p.10) onto non-stick paper. Leave until set.

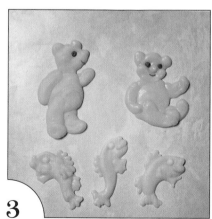

3
Repeat step 2 for the teddy bears and fishes using coloured white chocolate (see p.10).

54

4 Pipe shells around the cake-top edge (No.7).

5 Fix the boat and bears to the cake-top, then spread royal icing with a brush to create the sea.

6 Fix the fishes around the cake-side and ribbon around the board edge. Pipe inscription of choice (No.2) and fix candles as required.

TEMPLATES

OSCAR

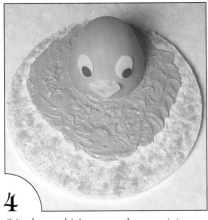

1 Cover a pudding basin shaped sponge with sugarpaste and place on a large board in position shown.

2 Cut out, shape and fix sugarpaste mouth and eyes.

3 Spread royal icing, using a small palette knife, onto the board to form the sea.

4 Stipple royal icing onto the remaining area of the board for the sand. Immediately sprinkle with demerara sugar.

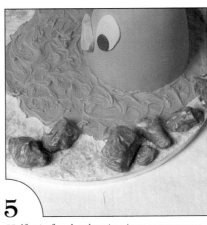

5 Half-mix food colouring into sugarpaste to make rocks. Fix to the sand.

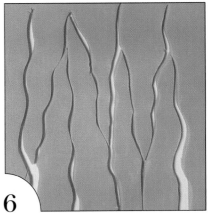

6 Roll out sugarpaste and cut into long, wavy lengths.

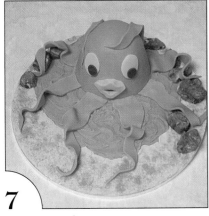

7 Immediately fix in various positions including two over the head.

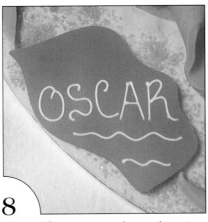

8 Cut and fix sugarpaste plaque, then pipe inscription of choice (No.1).

9 Make and fix sugarpaste sand-castles and decorate with flag. Fix party hat on head and ribbon around board.

CHIN CHIN

1
Using the template as a guide, cut out and fix sugarpaste ears and eyes onto a sugarpaste covered sponge.

2
Cut out and fix a sugarpaste nose. Then pipe mouth lines as shown (No.1).

3
Cut out and fix sugarpaste mouth, then pipe chin lines (No.1). Fix ribbon around base.

TEMPLATE

SCOTTY

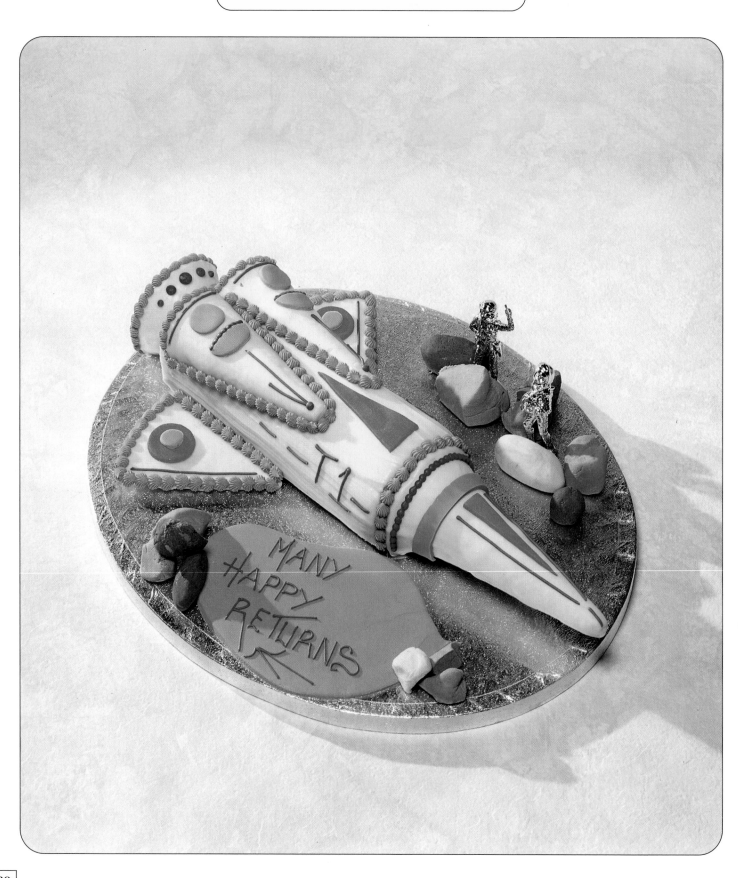

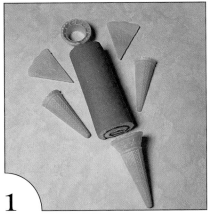

1

Gather together a swiss roll, ice cream cones and wafers as shown.

2

Melt white chocolate cake covering over hot water. Mix in food colouring of choice.

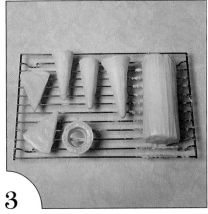

3

Then cover the swiss roll, cones and wafers with the melted chocolate. Leave to set.

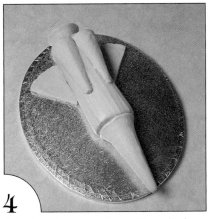

4

Join the pieces together, with melted chocolate, to form the rocket.

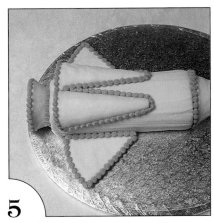

5

Pipe shells as shown with royal icing (No.42).

6

Cut out and fix the various sugarpaste shapes shown.

7

Pipe dots, numbers and lines as required (No.1).

8

Make and fix sugarpaste rocks around plastic space figures.

9

Cut out and fix a sugarpaste plaque. Pipe inscription of choice (No.1). Fix further rocks shown.

HECTOR

1 Cover a cake with sugarpaste. Then stipple royal icing around the board with a palette knife.

2 Cut out dinosaurs, scenery and plaque from modelling paste (see p.22). When dry and firm decorate the cut-outs and fix onto the cake-top and board.

3 Make multi-coloured rocks with sugarpaste and scatter around the cake-top and board. Fix ribbon around the board.

TEMPLATES

Apatosaurus

Camptosaurus

Stegasaurus

Tyrannosaurus

Brontosaurus

SILVIE

1 Cover a sponge with sugarpaste. When dry, pipe numerals around the cake-top edge (No.1), or draw the numerals using a confectioners' pen.

2 Cut out and fix sugarpaste pieces for eyes and cheeks. Using a sponge-stick (see index) dab food colouring for pupils. Pipe the mouth line (No.1).

3 Cut and fix hands in position at age of birthday. Fix ribbon around the base.

MARC

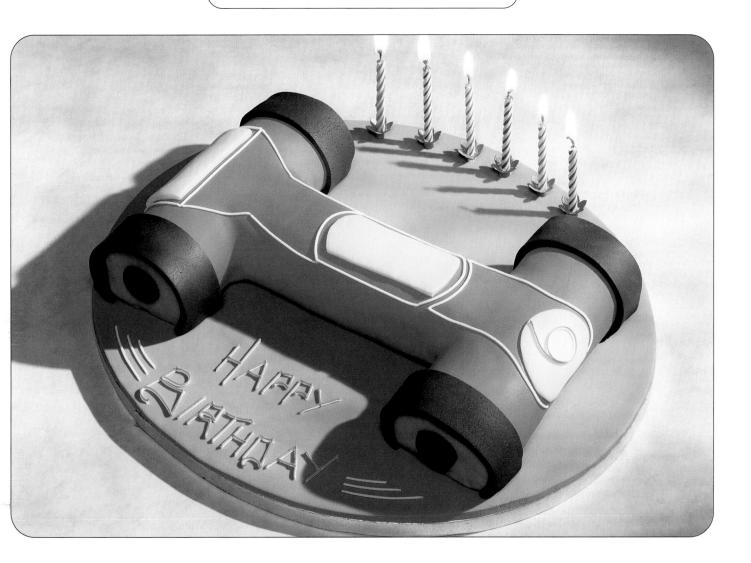

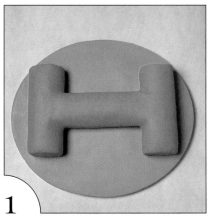

1 Cover a board with sugarpaste. Then cover three swiss rolls, placed in the position shown, with sugarpaste to form the car.

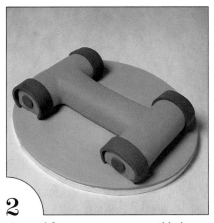

2 Cut and fix sugarpaste tyres and hubs.

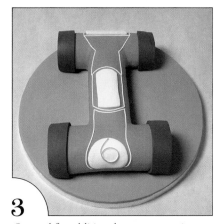

3 Cut and fix additional sugarpaste pieces shown. Then pipe the lines, number and inscription of choice (No.2) with royal icing. Fix candles as required.

GODFREY

1 Cover an oval cake board with sugarpaste or royal icing. Leave to dry for 24 hours, then cover sponge in sugarpaste and place at top of board.

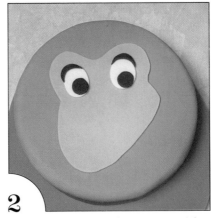

2 Using template as guide, cut out and fix sugarpaste head and eyes, as shown.

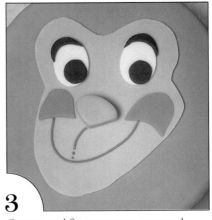

3 Cut out and fix sugarpaste nose and cheeks. Pipe the lines shown (No.2).

4

Spread royal icing or buttercream around the face. Brush surface to create fur effect.

5

Make and fix sugarpaste ears, then pipe the lines (No.1). Pipe tuft of hair at the top (No.3).

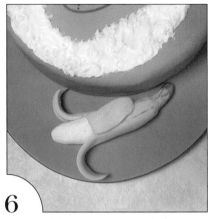

6

Make and fix a sugarpaste peeled banana onto the cake board.

TEMPLATE

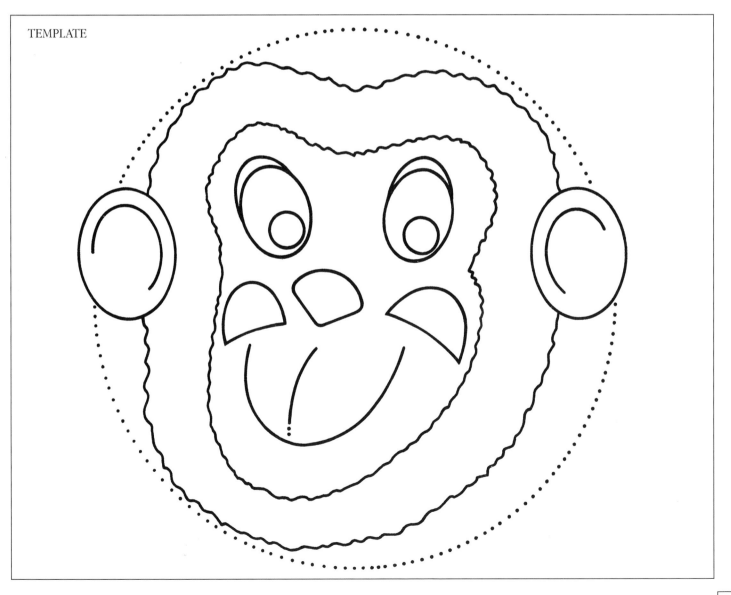

LAURIE

1
Cover a heart shaped board with sugarpaste and then, using heart shaped crimper, crimp the edge as shown. Fix ribbon around the cake board edge.

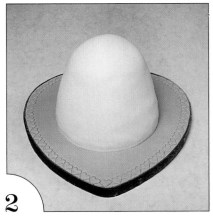

2
Cover a sponge cake, baked in an ovenproof basin, with sugarpaste and place centrally onto the board.

3
Pipe shells around the cake-base with royal icing (No.43).

4
Make and fix two layers of sugarpaste frills (see p.29) around the cake.

5
Pipe shells along the top-edge of the frill (No.2).

6
Cut out sugarpaste shapes using bright colours and fix as shown.

7
Dress a doll with sugarpaste as shown.

8
Cut and frill the edge of a sugarpaste disc and fix to the cake-top with the doll.

9
Make and fix, between the hands, an appropriate message on card.

CLAUDIO

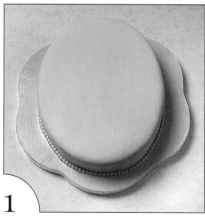

1 Sugarpaste an oval sponge and place onto a petal shaped board. Coat the board with royal icing. Leave to dry for 24 hours. Pipe shells around the base (No.3).

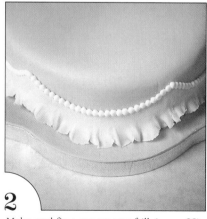

2 Make and fix a sugarpaste frill (see p.29) around the cake-side. Pipe shells along the join (No.2).

3 Using the template as a guide, cut out the pieces shown from sugarpaste and fix.

TEMPLATE

CARLY

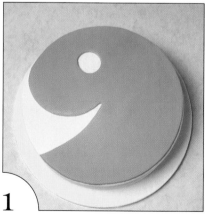

1

Coat a cake and board with royal icing, using a patterned scraper for the side. When dry, cut out and fix sugarpaste to the cake-top as shown.

2

Pipe shells around the cake-base and scrolls around the cake-top edge as shown (No.6) with royal icing.

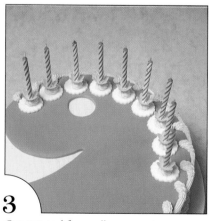

3

Cut out and fix small sugarpaste crimped circles. Then fix candles. Pipe inscription of choice (No.1). Fix ribbon and flowers as shown.

STAFFORD

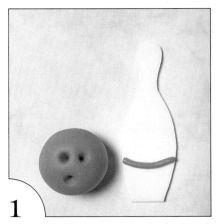

1 Cover an oblong sponge and cake board with sugarpaste. Mould a sugarpaste ball and cut out ten bowling pins. Pipe a line on each pin with royal icing (No.3).

2 When dry, place the pins and ball onto the cake-top as shown. Pipe shells around three edges (No.13).

3 Pipe a dot between each shell (No.2). Then pipe inscription of choice (No.1). Fix a ribbon around the cake-base.

BUPAH

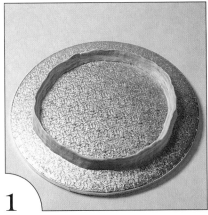

1 Make a triangular strip of sugarpaste and fix, as shown, onto a large cake board.

2 Cover the whole board with mottled sugarpaste (see p.11).

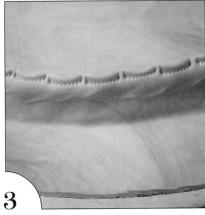

3 Immediately crimp the top-edge to form the pattern shown.

4 Cover a basin shaped sponge with sugarpaste and place into the centre of the board. Make and fix a sugarpaste rim around the base.

5 Cut and shape ice cream cones, then dip into melted chocolate (see p.10) and fix to the sugarpaste to form ears and nose.

6 Make and fix large sugarpaste eyes.

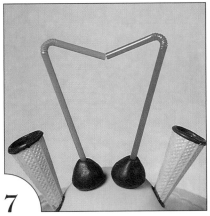

7 Make and fix two sugarpaste domes and fix plastic straws as shown.

8 Make and fix sugarpaste hands with long fingers.

9 Make and fix mottled sugarpaste rocks. Fix ribbon around the board.

CRISTY

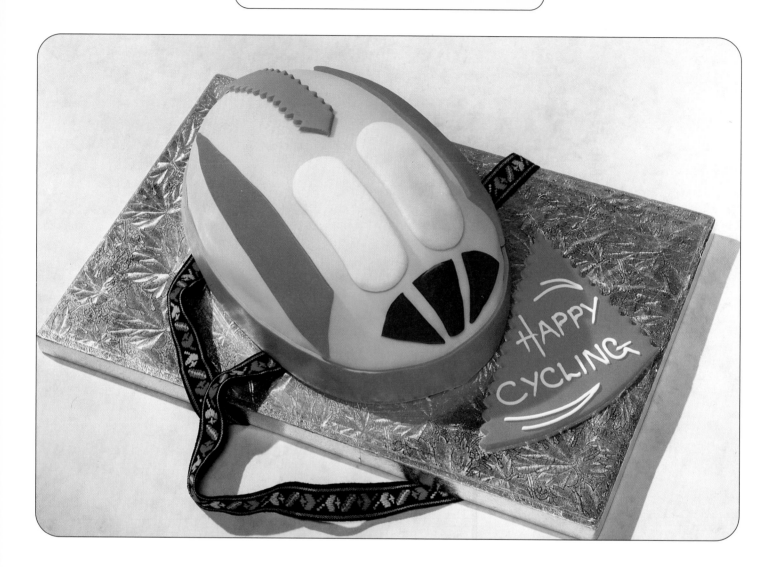

1 Cut a sponge to a cycle helmet shape, and cover with sugarpaste.

2 Cut out and fix sugarpaste shapes onto the helmet, to form a decorative and colourful design.

3 Cut out a sugarpaste plaque and pipe inscription of choice, with royal icing (No.2). Fix ribbon straps as shown.

MIKOL

1 Cut a square sponge in half, cream and fix together to form the shape shown. Cover with sugarpaste. Then cut out and fix sugarpaste pieces as shown.

2 Pipe the various lines shown with royal icing (No.1).

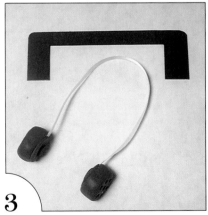

3 Make and fix a card handle. Then mould ear phones from sugarpaste and attach ribbon.

MARGAUX

1 Cover an hexagonal cake with sugarpaste and place onto the cake board. Then cover the board with pink and black sugarpaste as shown.

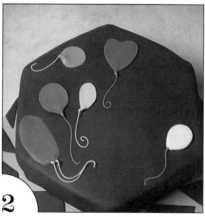

2 Cut out and fix sugarpaste balloons to the cake-top. Then pipe strings with royal icing (No.1).

3 Pipe recipient's name (No.2). Then fix ribbons around the cake-side and board.

LUCKY

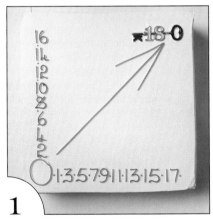

1 Coat a cake and board with royal icing. When dry, pipe numerals, dots and arrow with royal icing (No.1). Fix key as shown.

2 Pipe inscription of choice (No.1) then fix horseshoe and flowers.

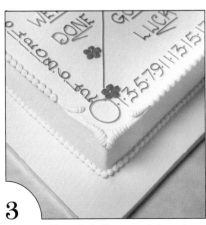

3 Pipe scrolls and shells around the cake-top edge and base (No.42). Pipe lines around the board edge (No.1). Fix decorations and ribbons.

KYLIE

1

Cover a cake and board with sugarpaste.
Crimp around the board edge. Pipe the
curved line shown with royal icing
(No.3).

2

Pipe a floral motif into each wide curve
(No's.2 and 1).

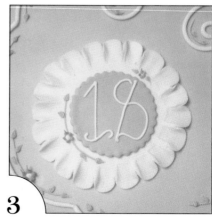

3

Make and fix a fluted sugarpaste plaque
to the cake-top and decorate as shown
(No.2). Fix ribbons and decorations of
choice.

ROCKIE

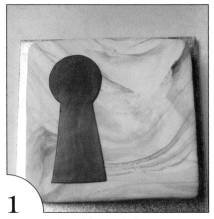

1
Cover a cake with mottled sugarpaste (see p.11). Then cut out and fix a sugarpaste keyhole to the cake-top.

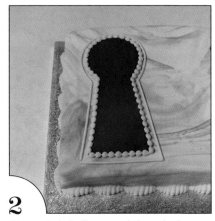

2
Pipe spiral shells around the cake-base and shells around the keyhole, with royal icing (No.42). Pipe a line beside the shells (No.2).

3
Pipe a scalloped line beside the line (No.1). Cut out and fix sugarpaste plaques, then pipe inscription (No.2). Fix decorations as required.

FREDDY

1 Cover a large round cake board with mottled sugarpaste (see p.11).

2 Roll out and cut a sugarpaste lily leaf and place onto a medium sized board. Frill the edge, then mark veins with a bone tool.

3 Carefully slide the leaf off the board and onto the mottled sugarpaste. Leave to dry for 24 hours.

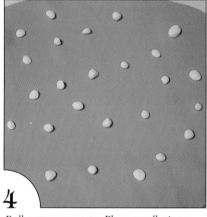

4 Roll out sugarpaste. Place small pieces on top, roll again to form pattern. Cover with polythene.

5 Fix two pieces of sponge onto a basin shaped sponge, to form mounds for eyes. Immediately cover the sponge with the sugarpaste.

6 Place the sponge onto the lily leaf. Make and fix sugarpaste feet and hands.

7 Mould and fix two sugarpaste eyes.

8 Pipe the mouth lines with royal icing (No.3). Make and fix a curled sugarpaste tongue.

9 Pipe inscription of choice with royal icing (No.2).

1 Cover a cake with almond paste (see p.25). Then cover the top only with sugarpaste.

2 Cut out two greaseproof paper discs and place one onto the cake-top. Fold the second disc into eight sections.

3 Cover the cake-top with a second layer of sugarpaste (fixing to the first layer, not to the paper).

4 Immediately cover the whole cake and board with sugarpaste.

5 Unfold the second paper disc and place onto the cake-top. Using the disc as a guide, mark the sugarpaste for cutting.

6 Remove the disc then cut the first two layers of sugarpaste and fold each leaf outwards as shown. Then remove the paper disc.

7 Pipe numerals (No.2) and inscription (No.1) with royal icing. Make and fix ribbon bows.

8 Pipe spiral shells around the cake-base (No.7). Then pipe the dots as shown (No.1).

9 Decorate a doll with a sugarpaste dress, bow and feather. Fix to the cake-top. Fix leaves and ribbon around the cake board edge.

BECKY

1 Coat the cake and board with royal icing. When dry, stipple royal icing around the cake-top edge and board, as shown.

2 Using the templates as a guide, cut out sugarpaste pieces for all the tortoises required.

3 Fix the large tortoise pieces to the cake-top as shown.

4

Fix the smaller tortoises around the cake-sides and pipe grass with royal icing (No.1).

5

Pipe inscription of choice and decorate with tracery (No.1).

6

Pipe shells around part of the cake-top edge (No.42). Pipe a line over the shells (No.1). Fix ribbon around the board.

TEMPLATES

VANCE

1 Using the template as a guide, cut out and fix sugarpaste pieces onto a cake coated with royal icing.

2 Decorate the artist and painting with royal icing, as shown.

3 Pipe shells around the cake-top edge and base (No.3). Pipe a line over the cake-base shells (No.2). Then overpipe the line (No.1). Fix the paint brush and motif.

TEMPLATES

MERLIN

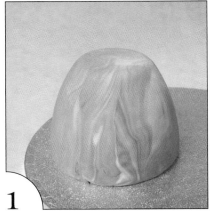

1 Cover a basin shaped sponge, with mottled sugarpaste (see p.11). Then place onto an oval cake board.

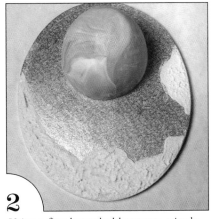

2 Using a fine household sponge, stipple the board with royal icing to resemble sand as shown.

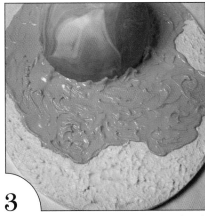

3 Spread royal icing between the sand and the cake with a palette knife, to resemble the sea.

4 Make a mermaid's tail with sugarpaste and mark scales with a small cutter. Insert the body and place on a basin to dry.

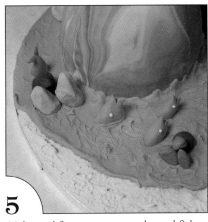

5 Make and fix sugarpaste rocks and fish as shown.

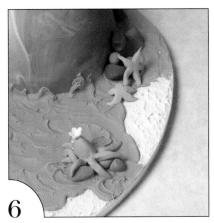

6 Make and fix further sugarpaste rocks, octopus and star fish as shown.

7 Fix the mermaid to the cake-top.

8 Make and fix sugarpaste sand-castles and shell. Make and insert flags as required.

9 Pipe inscription of choice with royal icing (No.1) onto the shell. Fix a ribbon bow.

LYNETTE

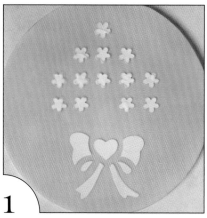

1 Cover a sponge and board with sugarpaste. Make a stencil from page 40, place onto cake-top and spread over with royal icing (see p.46).

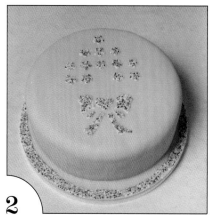

2 Immediately sprinkle hundreds and thousands over the icing, then remove the stencils. Spread icing around the board and sprinkle with hundreds and thousands.

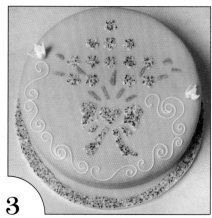

3 Pipe curved lines as shown (No.2). Cut and fix jelly diamond, stalks and leaves. Fix decorations of choice and ribbon around the cake-base.

ANDIE

1
Cover the cake-top with almond paste and royal icing. When dry spread additional royal icing across half the top, using a serrated scraper.

2
Using templates from page 103 as a guide, cut out sugarpaste anchor and life belts. Pipe ropes with royal icing (No.2) and fix to the cake-top.

3
Pipe inscription of choice as shown (No.2). Pipe shells and scrolls around the cake-top edge (No.7). Fix band around the cake-side.

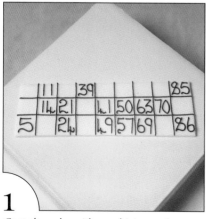

1 Coat the cake with royal icing, using a patterned scraper for the sides. When dry make and fix a sugarpaste bingo card. Pipe the lines and numbers (No.1).

2 Pipe inscription of choice and caller's quotes, as shown (No.1).

3 Pipe shells and scrolls around the cake-top edge and base (No.42). Make and fix a sugarpaste pencil. Pipe "BINGO" (No.1) and fix flowers as required.

CHARLES

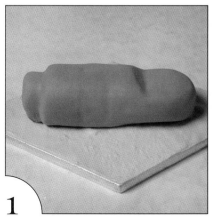

1 Stipple the cake board with royal icing. Cut a swiss roll to golf bag shape and cover with sugarpaste. Then place onto the board.

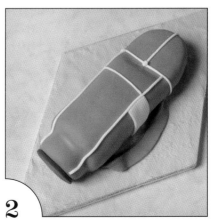

2 Cut and fix a sugarpaste handle, side pieces and a base. Pipe the lines shown (No.2) with royal icing.

3 Pipe inscription of choice (No.1). Make and fix sugarpaste golf balls and tees.

FELIX

1 Cover an oval cake and board with sugarpaste.

2 Using the template as a guide, cut out and fix the shape shown (extending down the cake-side and onto the board).

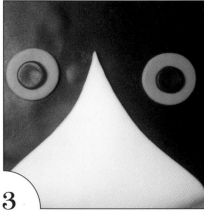

3 Cut out and fix the eyes from sugarpaste.

4 Cut out, and fix together, two pairs of sugarpaste circles. Fold over and fix to the cake-top to form ears.

5 Make and fix a sugarpaste nose. Then pipe the mouth with royal icing (No.1).

6 Cut lengths of spaghetti and push into the sugarpaste to form whiskers.

TEMPLATE

LOVE

1 Sugarpaste the cake-top and immediately crimp the edge. Then cut out, frill and fix a sugarpaste ribbon. Pipe inscription with royal icing (No.1).

2 Cut out, frill and fix a sugarpaste heart. Decorate as required.

3 Cut out and fix sugarpaste flowers. Pipe leaves (No.1). Fix decorative band around the cake-side.

CAMILLE

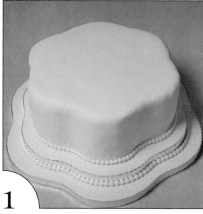

1 Cover a sponge with sugarpaste and place onto two cake boards fixed together. Spread royal icing over the boards, then pipe shells as shown (No.3).

2 Place a patterned doyley onto the cake-top and spread royal icing over it thinly. Then remove the doyley in one continuous movement.

3 When dry, fix a variety of decorations on to the cake-top and around the sides.

CAPRICORN

1 Using the template as a guide and two colours of sugarpaste, cut out the goat as shown.

2 Coat an oval cake and board with royal icing, using a comb scraper for the cake-side. When dry, fix the goat onto the cake-top. Make and fix sugarpaste horns.

3 Brush royal icing over the front body to form the hair. Then pipe facial features and curved lines on the tail to form scales (No.1).

4 Pipe inscription of choice (No.1). Then pipe small scrolls under the inscription (No.1).

5 Cut out and fix a strip of sugarpaste to represent a mountain stream.

6 Cut out and fix sugarpaste strips to represent mountain rocks, as shown. Pipe shells on remaining cake-top edge and base (No.44).

TEMPLATE

AQUARIUS

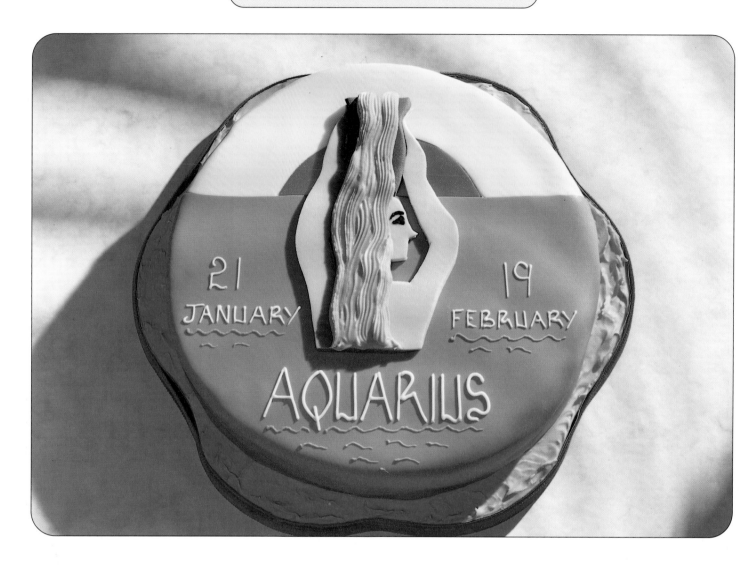

1 Cover a sponge with various shapes and colours of sugarpaste, then place onto a petal shaped cake board. Stipple the board with royal icing.

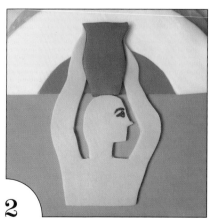

2 Using the template as a guide, cut out and fix sugarpaste figure and vase.

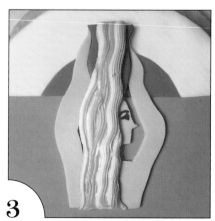

3 Pipe wavy lines with royal icing (No.44), using two colours in the piping bag, to form water. Pipe and decorate inscription of choice (No.1).

TEMPLATES

PISCES

1

Cover cake board with mottled sugarpaste (see p.11) in colours shown. Leave to dry for 24 hours.

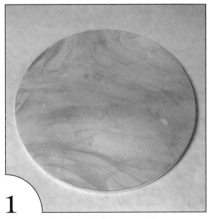

2

Using the template as a guide, cut a round sponge in half along the dotted line. Cover with sugarpaste and place onto the board.

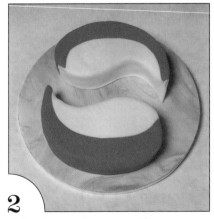

3

Cut out and fix sugarpaste eyes and mouths.

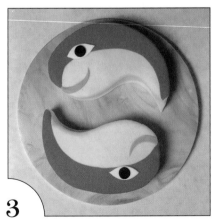

4 Trace fins and tails onto rice paper using a confectioners' pen. Cut out and fix to the fishes as shown.

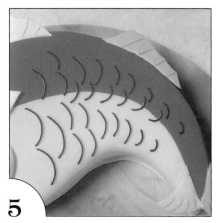

5 Pipe curved lines with royal icing (No.1), to represent fish scales.

6 Pipe inscription of choice (No.1) between the fish, and around the cake board edge.

TEMPLATES

Cut along line

ARIES

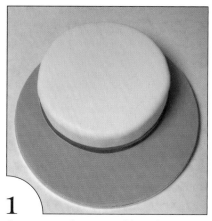

1
Sugarpaste a large round board. Leave to dry for 24 hours. Then sugarpaste a sponge and place onto the board in the position shown. Fix ribbon around the cake-base.

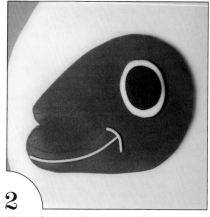

2
Using the template as a guide, cut out and fix a sugarpaste head and eye. Pipe the mouth with royal icing (No.2).

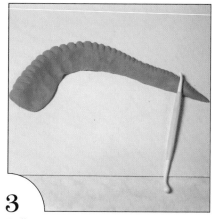

3
Roll out sugarpaste to a triangular shape, flatten lower edge then mark upper edge with a bone tool.

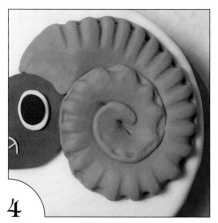

4 Roll-up the triangle to form the horn and fix onto the cake-top as shown.

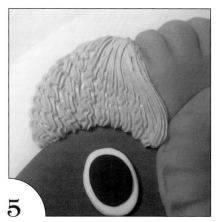

5 Pipe the forehead using royal icing (No.7).

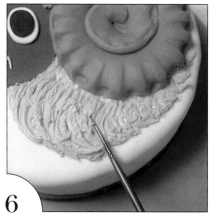

6 Spread royal icing, using a palette knife, below the face and horn and then stroke with a paintbrush to form hair. Pipe inscription of choice (No.2).

TEMPLATE

TAURUS

1

Using template as guide, cut, then cover, sponge with sugarpaste. Place onto a cake board. Stipple remaining board surface with royal icing, as shown.

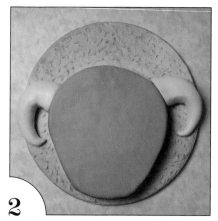

2

When the royal icing is dry, mould sugarpaste into curved horns and fix in position.

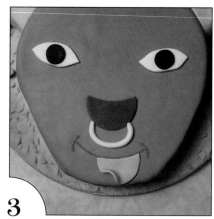

3

Cut out and fix sugarpaste eyes, nose and ring. Pipe the mouth (No.1). Cut and fix a sugarpaste tongue.

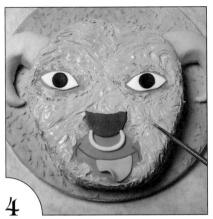

4 Spread royal icing over the face, then brush to form hair.

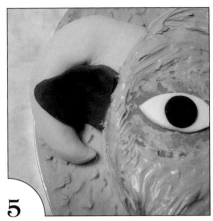

5 Cut and fix a sugarpaste ear below each horn.

6 Cut and place a sugarpaste plaque to the top of the cake board and pipe inscription of choice (No.1).

TEMPLATES

GEMINI

1
Sugarpaste a square cake board. Leave
to dry for 24 hours. Sugarpaste two
round sponges (one cut to fit) and place
onto the board as shown.

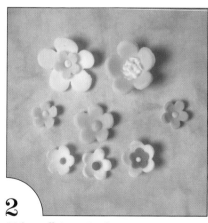

2
Make sufficient simple sugarpaste
flowers to decorate the cake. Leave until
dry.

3
Cut out and fix sugarpaste eyes. Pipe
nostrils and mouths (one smiling and
one sad) with royal icing (No.1).

4
Brush royal icing to form hair in the style and colour shown.

5
Pipe inscription of choice with royal icing (No.1).

6
Fix the sugarpaste flowers around the cake board, then fix bows under each chin, as shown.

TEMPLATE

CANCER

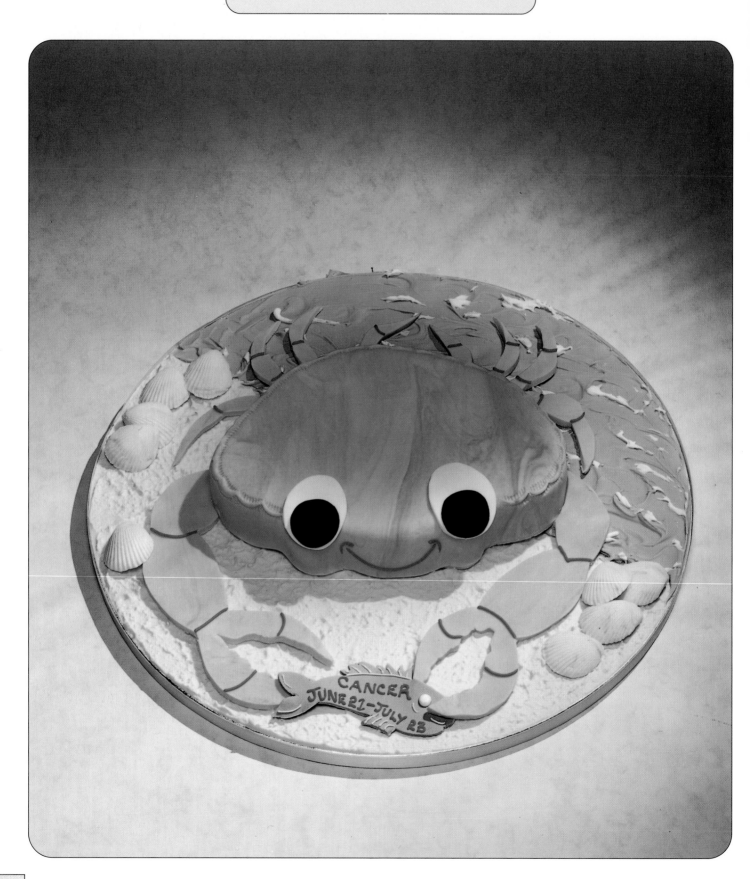

1 Spread sea-coloured royal icing over part of the cake board, using a palette knife to create waves. Then stipple sand-coloured royal icing over remaining surface.

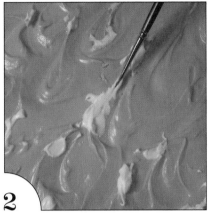

2 Using a small paint brush, dab white royal icing onto the tops of the waves, as shown. Leave to dry for 24 hours.

3 Using the template as a guide, cut sponge to body shape. Cover with sugarpaste, crimp the edge as shown then place onto the cake board.

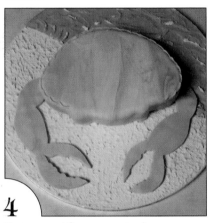

4 Cut out and fix sugarpaste claws.

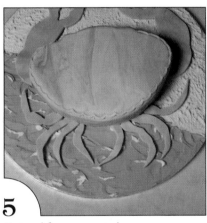

5 Cut and fix sugarpaste legs.

6 Pipe the joint lines with royal icing (No.1).

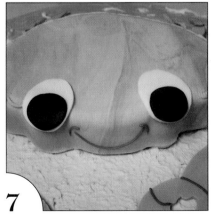

7 Cut out and fix sugarpaste eyes. Then pipe the mouth (No.1).

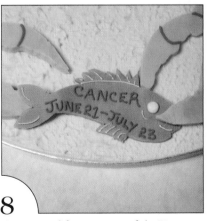

8 Cut out and fix sugarpaste fish. Pipe inscription of choice and decorate (No.1).

9 Press mottled sugarpaste into a real sea-shell, gently peel out and place as required.

TEMPLATES

LEO

1
Sugarpaste a round sponge and place onto a board in the position shown. Using two colours of royal icing, stipple the remaining surface of the board.

2
Using the template as a guide, make and fix a flat shaped wedge of sugarpaste to the cake-top.

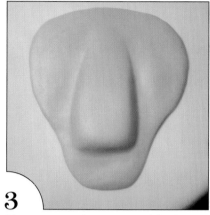

3
Using sugarpaste, cut out and fix the face over the wedge as shown.

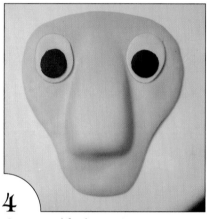

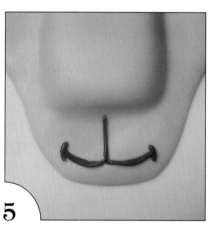

4
Cut out and fix the sugarpaste eyes.

5
Using royal icing, pipe the mouth as shown (No.2).

6
Spread royal icing from the face to the cake-top edge. Then immediately fork the icing, in the directions shown, to form hair.

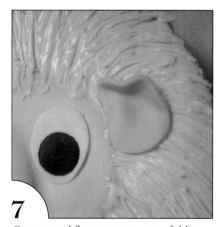

7
Cut out and fix sugarpaste ears, folding as shown.

8
Pipe elongated star shapes (No.7) around the cake-base with royal icing

9
Cut out and fix sugarpaste leaves onto the cake board. Then pipe inscription of choice (No.1).

TEMPLATE

VIRGO

1 Pipe sufficient flowers with royal icing (No's.57 and 1), to line the cake-base and part of the cake-top edge. Leave to dry for 24 hours.

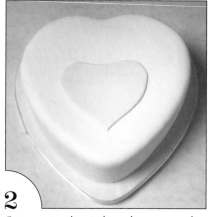

2 Sugarpaste a heart shaped sponge and board as shown. Using the template as a guide, cut and fix the sugarpaste head.

3 Cut and fix sugarpaste eyes and mouth. Then pipe dots for the nose (No.1).

4 Spread royal icing around the head, then brush to form hair. Fix a small bow in position shown.

5 Pipe inscription of choice (No.1). Then pipe small scrolls and tracery to decorate the inscription (No.1).

6 Fix the piped sugar flowers around the cake-top edge and base. Fix ribbon around the cake-side.

TEMPLATE

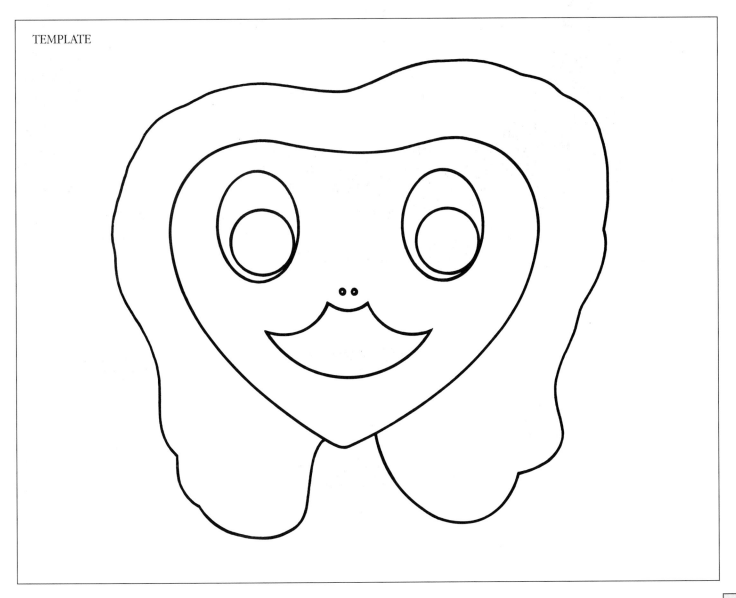

LIBRA

1 Cover cake and board with sugarpaste, then immediately crimp the edge, as shown.

2 Using the template as a guide, cut out and fix sugarpaste support and scales.

3 Decorate with piped shells and lines, using royal icing (No.1). Then pipe inscription (No.1). Fix sugar birds and silk flowers.

TEMPLATES

SCORPIO

1

Using a palette knife, spread royal icing of various colours onto an oblong cake board. Leave to dry for 24 hours.

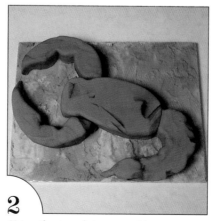

2

Using the template as a guide, cut out sponge cake body, tail and claws. Cover with mottled sugarpaste (see p.11) and place onto the board.

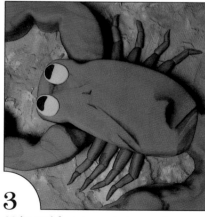

3

Make and fix sugarpaste legs and eyes. Pipe inscription of choice with royal icing (No.1).

TEMPLATE

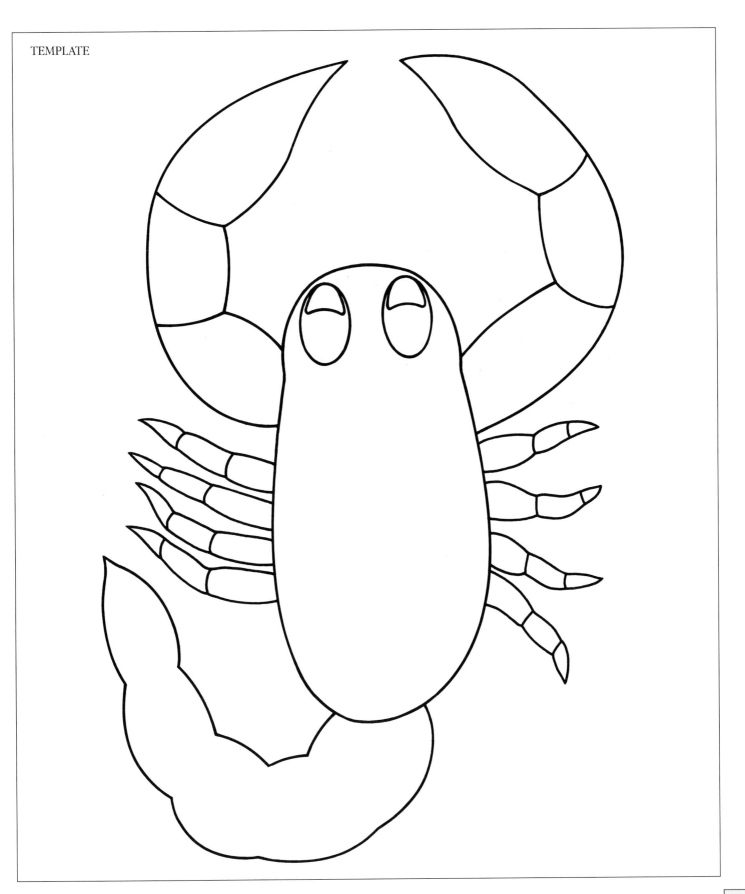

SAGITTARIUS

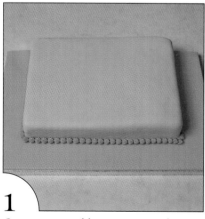

1 Sugarpaste an oblong sponge and board. Leave to dry for 24 hours. Then pipe shells with royal icing around the base (No.44).

2 Roll out two colours of sugarpaste as shown.

3 Using the template as a guide, cut out the archer as shown.

4 Fix the archer to the cake-top, then pipe the hair, facial features and body lines (No.1).

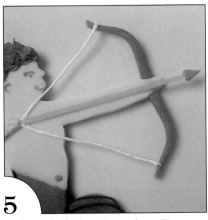

5 Make and fix a sugarpaste bow. Fix edible string and a stick of spaghetti for arrow. Pipe the arrow head with royal icing (No.1).

6 Pipe inscription of choice onto the cake board (No.1). Fix artificial flowers as required.

TEMPLATE

MOIRA

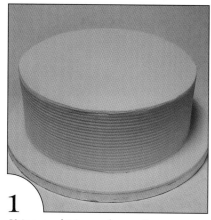

1 Using royal icing and a comb scraper, create pattern shown on the cake-side. Leave to dry for 24 hours.

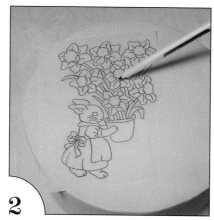

2 Trace template onto greaseproof paper and transfer design onto the cake-top (see index).

3 Pipe over the lines of the design with royal icing (No.1).

4 Fill-in the flowers and pot with piping gel, using a variety of colours (see p.10).

5 Fill-in the rabbit with piping gel, using a variety of colours.

6 Pipe shells around the cake-top and base (No.44). Pipe inscription of choice (No.1). Fix ribbon around the cake-side and board edge.

TEMPLATES

DARREN

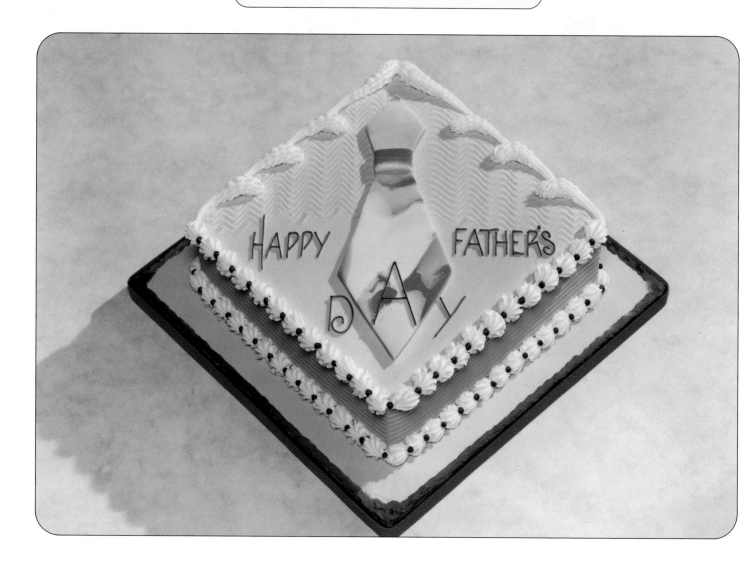

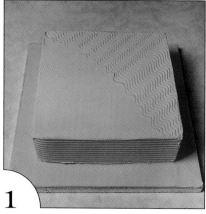

1 Coat the cake with royal icing, using a comb scraper across half the cake-top and around the sides on the final coat, as shown. Then coat the board.

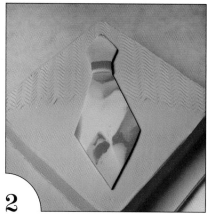

2 When the icing is dry, cut out and fix a mottled sugarpaste tie, using the template as a guide.

3 Pipe inscription of choice with royal icing (No.1) as shown.

4 Pipe scrolls around two sides of the cake-top edge (No.7).

5 Pipe shells around the remaining cake-top edges, then around the cake-base (No.7).

6 Pipe a dot between each shell (No.2). Then stipple royal icing along the perimeter of the cake. Fix ribbon around the cake board edge.

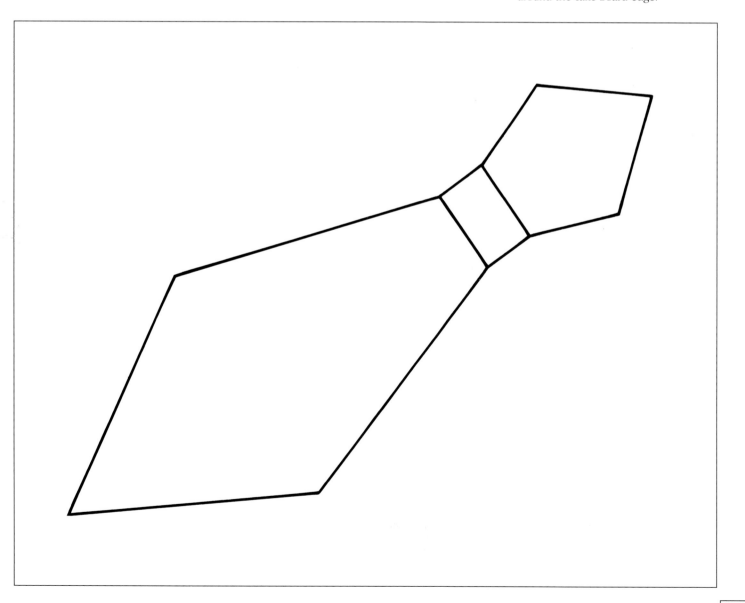

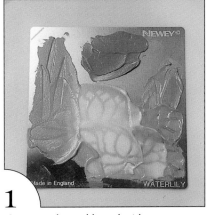

1
Cover a cake and board with sugarpaste. Crimp edges. Using templates on p.132, cut stencils (see index). Spread softened royal icing over stencil as shown.

2
Scrape the surplus icing off the stencil with a palette knife held flat. Then carefully lift the template away in one continuous movement.

3
Pipe inscription of choice (No.1). Then decorate the cake with tracery and graduated dots (No.1). Then fix ribbons and bows as shown.

FLORIA

1 Cover the cake and board with sugarpaste. Crimp around the board edge. When dry follow steps 1-2 on p.130 to form patterns shown. (Templates are on p.132.)

2 Pipe scrolls and shells around the cake-top edge and base with royal icing (No.42).

3 Pipe curved lines beside the scrolls (No.2). Pipe inscription of choice and decorate (No.1). Fix bows and sugar birds as shown.

TEMPLATES

ACE

1 Cover the cake-top with almond paste, then sugarpaste. Fix additional strips of sugarpaste around the cake-top edge.

2 Make and decorate modelling paste (see p.22) cards as shown.

3 Make and fix a sugarpaste pencil and plaque. Pipe inscription of choice (No.1). Fix band around the cake-side.

MANDIE

1 Cut and shape sponges to form an open book. Place onto a cake board and coat the sponge with buttercream.

2 Cover the book with sugarpaste and then mark the edges with the back of a knife, to create pages.

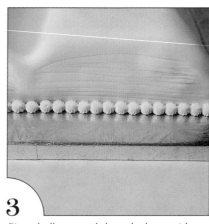

3 Pipe shells around the cake-base with royal icing (No.44).

4 Using the templates as a guide, cut out and fix sugarpaste cross and plaque. Cut and fix ribbon book-mark as shown.

5 Pipe the name required (No.1) then decorate the cross with piping and tracery (No.1). Fix small flowers as shown.

6 Pipe the message and date (No.1) then decorate with piped tracery (No.1). Fix small flowers as shown.

TEMPLATES

ESTA

1
Coat one layer of sponge with buttercream, place a second sponge (with centre cut out) on top and coat with buttercream.

2
Cover top and side with grated chocolate (avoid the centre if possible).

3
Cover the centre with grated white chocolate. Spread buttercream around the cake board and cover with coloured coconut.

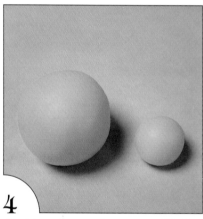

4
Mould two large and twenty small balls from almond paste to form chicks heads.

5
Cut out almond paste diamond shapes and fix to the heads, using the blunt end of a paintbrush to form beaks.

6
Make and fix almond paste hats as shown. Then pipe eyes with royal icing (No.1).

7
Cut out and fix almond paste combs. Pipe the eyes (No.1).

8
Mould two almond paste balls to form bodies and place in centre, as shown, then fix on the heads.

9
Fix the small heads around the cake board and a ribbon around the cake board edge.

DANNY

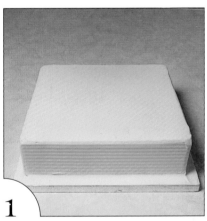

1 Coat the cake and board with royal icing, using a comb scraper for the cake-sides. Leave to dry for 24 hours.

2 Using the templates as a guide, cut out sugarpaste domino shapes. Immediately indent dots for appropriate numbers using a bone tool.

3 Pipe a dot into each indentation with royal icing (No.2).

4
Place the dominoes onto the cake-top, ensuring the numbers match at the joins. The total should add up to the retirement age.

5
Pipe inscription of choice (No.1) in the manner shown.

6
Pipe scrolls down the cake-top edge as shown (No.7).

7
Pipe shells around the remaining cake-top edges and base (No.7).

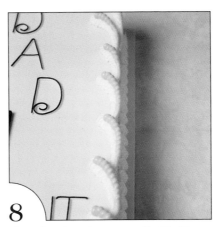

8
Overpipe the cake-top scrolls (No.3).

9
Pipe a dot between each shell using the colours of the dominoes (No.2).

TEMPLATES

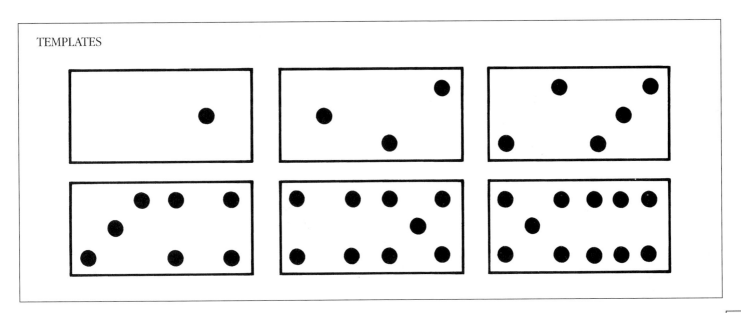

TRISHA

1 Cover cake and board with sugarpaste. Crimp the board edge. Using template as a guide, cut out and fix a raised umbrella top. Support, if necessary, with sugarpaste.

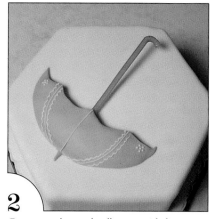

2 Decorate the umbrella top with lines piped with royal icing (No.1). Cut and fix a plastic straw handle.

3 Fill the umbrella with flowers, ribbon loops and bows.

4 Make and decorate a small umbrella for each cake-side as shown.

5 Pipe inscription of choice around the cake-top edge (No.1).

6 Pipe shells around the cake-base (No.2). Then pipe a line over the shells (No.1).

TEMPLATES

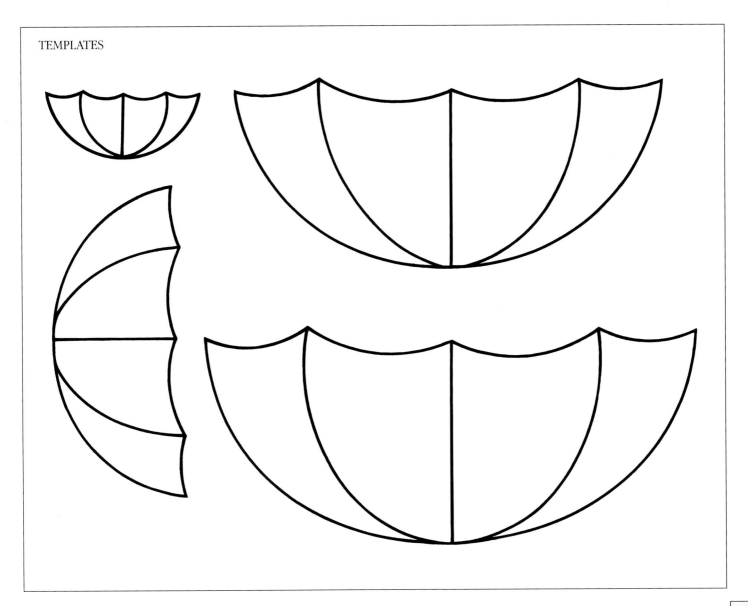

FRANCIS

1
Spread buttercream over a swiss roll. Then cover each end with a disc of sugarpaste.

2
Roll out a long sheet of sugarpaste the same width as the roll. Place the roll at the top end.

3
Roll up the swiss roll using all the sugarpaste. Turn the roll over and carefully unwind some of the sugarpaste to form the scroll.

4

Lightly stipple the sides with royal icing, using a fine household sponge.

5

Pipe message of choice (No.1) then decorate with tracery (No.1).

6

Cut out and fix sugarpaste leaves and flowers as shown. Make and fix a ribbon bow.

TEMPLATE

LYNDY

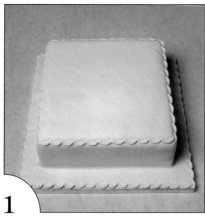

1 Cover the cake and board with sugarpaste and immediately crimp the cake-top edge and board edge as shown.

2 Using the template as a guide, cut out the horseshoe and cat from sugarpaste. Fix to the cake-top.

3 Pipe inscription of choice (No.1) with royal icing.

4 Pipe the floral motif as shown (No.1).

5 Pipe a scalloped line around the cake-sides (No.1).

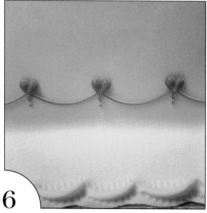

6 Pipe two elongated shells at each curved join (No.1). Pipe a flower at each board corner. Fix a ribbon bow to the cake-top.

TEMPLATES

WHITNEY

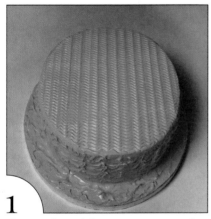

1 Coat a cake with buttercream, or royal icing, using a serrated scraper for the cake-top and a palette knife around the sides and board.

2 Using sugarpaste, cut out and fix the shape of Great Britain to the cake-top.

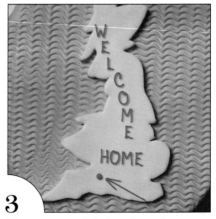

3 Pipe message of choice, dot and arrow to indicate place of residence (No.1). Fix toys and flag as required.

VALENTINA

1 Cover the cake and board with sugarpaste. Immediately crimp the sugarpaste around the board edge. Cut out and fix a sugarpaste double heart onto the cake-top.

2 Cut out and fix a sugarpaste ribbon onto the hearts. Pipe inscription of choice with royal icing (No.1).

3 Pipe the tracery shown (No.2). Fix decorations and ribbons of choice.

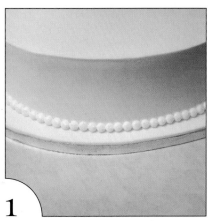

1
Using royal icing, pipe shells (No.3) around the base of a cake coated with royal icing.

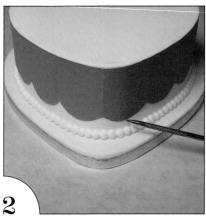

2
Fold a length of paper, equal to the diameter of the cake, into equal divisions. Cut a curve, unfold and mark cake-side as shown.

3
Pipe a frill (No.59) following the marked line around the cake-side.

4

Pipe another frill above the first frill (No.59).

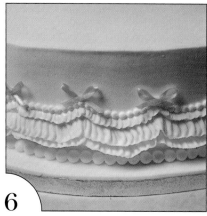

5

Pipe another frill above the last frill (No.57).

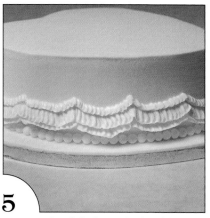

6

Pipe shells along the top-edge of the frill (No.2). Make and fix a ribbon bow against the top of each curve.

7

Mark the cake-top edge into divisions following the same points as the cake-side positions. Pipe a frill (No.59) as shown.

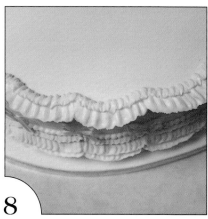

8

Pipe a frill against the first frill (No.57).

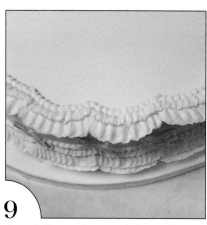

9

Pipe shells (No.2) around the inside-edge.

10

Pipe inscription of choice (No.2).

11

Overpipe the inscription (No.1), then pipe tracery to decorate (No.1).

12

Make and fix a floral spray, appropriate motifs and ribbon bows.

HEIDI

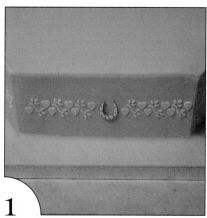

1 Coat an hexagonal cake and board with royal icing. Leave to dry for 24 hours. Stencil each cake-side as shown (see p.46 and index). Fix horseshoes in centres.

2 Stencil the cake-top with patterns shown.

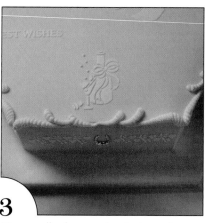

3 Pipe scrolls along each cake-top edge with royal icing (No.42).

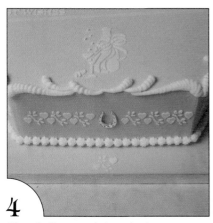

4 Pipe shells around the cake-base (No.42). Then stencil the pattern shown around the cake board.

5 Overpipe the scrolls (No.2). Then pipe tracery to decorate the inscription (No.1).

6 Pipe a line over each shell (No.2). Pipe scrolls around the cake board edge (No.1).

TEMPLATES

NINETTE

1 Bake a cake in a 2pt ovenproof basin. Cut in half and cover with sugarpaste. Then make 2 templates from card and place onto the cake board as shown.

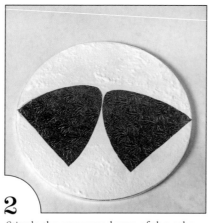

2 Stipple the uncovered area of the cake board with royal icing, then carefully remove the card templates.

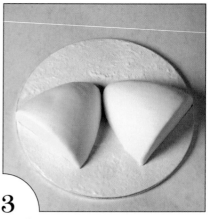

3 Carefully place the cakes onto the cake board.

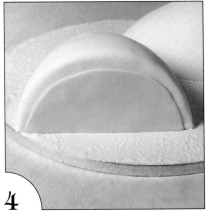

4 Cut out and fix sugarpaste to each bell end in the shape shown.

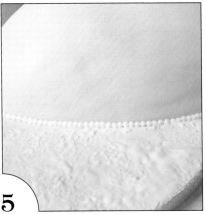

5 Pipe shells around the cake-bases with royal icing (No.2).

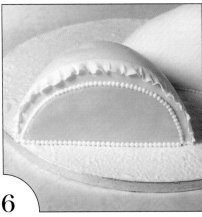

6 Pipe shells around the edge of each cut-out. Make and fix a sugarpaste frilled band to each cake-top edge (see p.29).

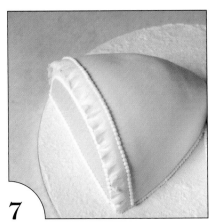

7 Pipe shells along the edge of each band (No.2).

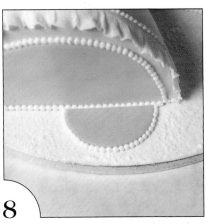

8 Cut out and fix a sugarpaste semi-circle to represent the clangers. Pipe shells around the edges as shown (No.2).

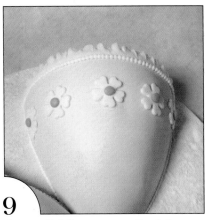

9 Cut out and fix sugarpaste floral shapes over the cake-tops. Then pipe the flower centres (No.3).

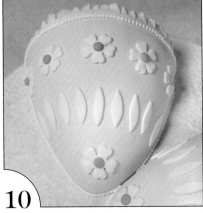

10 Repeat step 9 at the end of each bell. Then cut out and fix the oval shapes shown from sugarpaste.

11 Cut out and fix a sugarpaste plaque. Then pipe inscription of choice and tracery (No.1). Fix decorations as required.

12 Make and fix ribbon loops and string pearls to join the bells together. Then decorate with small ribbon bows.

ZOLA

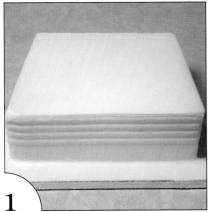

1

Coat cakes with royal icing using a patterned scraper for the sides. Then coat the board. Leave to dry for 24 hours.

2

Pipe a quantity of sugar flowers (No.57). Then pipe the centres (No.1). Leave to dry for 24 hours.

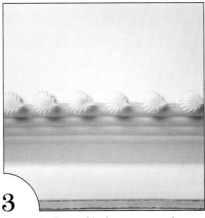

3

Pipe a shell (No.44), leave an equal space, pipe another shell then repeat the process around the cake-top edge.

4

Fix the sugar flowers between the shells.

5

Repeat steps 3 and 4 around the cake-base.

6

Make and fix a ribbon bow to each cake-side and decorate each with a sugar flower.

7

Fix a horseshoe at each corner of the board and decorate with a ribbon bow and sugar flower.

8

Fix and decorate horseshoes to the centre of the bottom tier as shown.

9

Place the pillars in position and pipe shells around the bases (No.42). Decorate with ribbon bow and sugar flower.

TONI

1 Using royal icing, pipe shells (No.44) around the base of cakes coated with royal icing.

2 Gather and secure lace banding around the middle of the cake side.

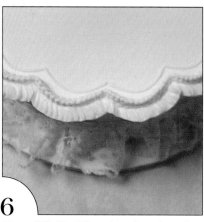

3 Fold a circle of paper, the diameter of the cake-top, into 16. Mark the cake and pipe scalloped rope (No.44) as shown.

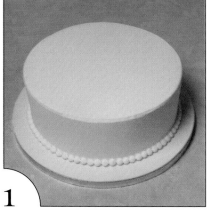

4 Overpipe the rope (No.3).

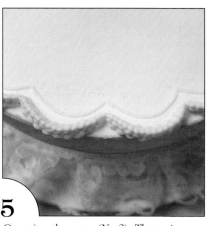

5 Overpipe the rope (No.2). Then pipe curved lines beside the rope (No.2).

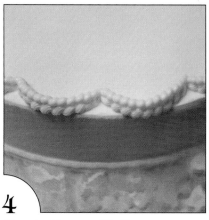

6 Pipe a frill (No.59) against the edge of the rope, keeping the piping tube horizontal.

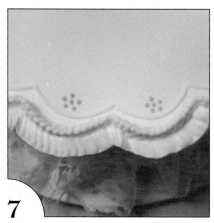

7 Pipe dots in each curve (No.1).

8 Make and fix ribbon bows around the cake-side.

9 Make and fix ribbon spray and horseshoe to centre of bottom and middle tier.

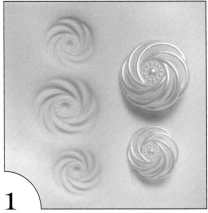

1
Cover the cake with sugarpaste and immediately press a large and small button into the cake-side to form the pattern shown.

2
Pipe shells around the cake-base (No.43) with royal icing.

3
Pipe various scrolls around the cake-top edge (No.43).

4
Pipe floral motifs, as shown, around the cake-side (No.1).

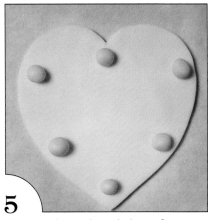

5
Cut out a heart-shaped plaque from sugarpaste. Then mould and fix sugarpaste balls.

6
Immediately press a button onto each ball to form the floral design shown.

7
Fix the plaque to the cake-top and pipe shells (No.43) around the edge. Fix a motif of choice to the plaque.

8
Pipe a floral design around the heart-shaped plaque (No.1).

9
Pipe a floral design beside the cake-top scrolls (No.1). Fix decorations of choice.

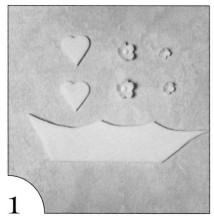

1 Cut out sugarpaste corner shapes of appropriate sizes to fit the cakes. Cut out heart shapes and flowers as shown.

2 Place the cakes onto the boards, then fix the sugarpaste corner pieces.

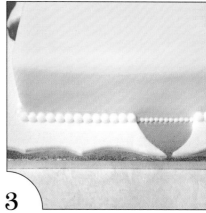

3 Pipe shells along the cake-base centres with royal icing (No.1). Then pipe shells along the corner pieces (No.3).

4 Pipe curved lines as shown (No.2) around the cake-top edge.

5 Fix the hearts and flowers against the piped lines.

6 Decorate the cake boards with hearts, flowers and horseshoes. Fix ribbons and decorations as required.

TEMPLATES

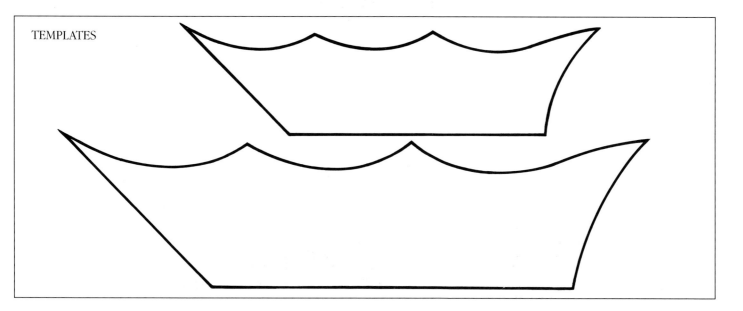

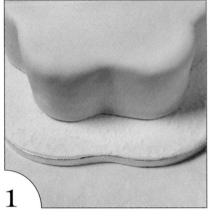

1
Cover petal-shaped cakes with sugarpaste. Place onto cake boards then stipple royal icing around each board. Leave to dry for 24 hours.

2
Pipe bells onto non-stick paper using royal icing without glycerin (No.3). Sprinkle sugar over the bells, then leave until outside has formed a crust.

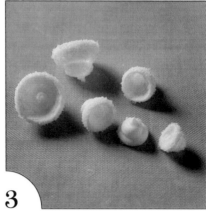

3
Carefully lift the bells off the paper and scoop out the soft icing, to form the bells. Leave until dry.

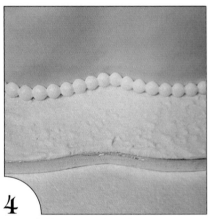

4
Pipe shells around the cake-bases (No.3).

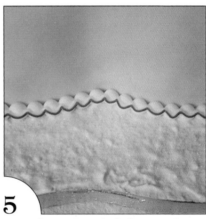

5
Pipe a line over each shell (No.2) then overpipe the line (No.1).

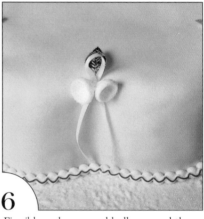

6
Fix ribbon, leaves and bells around the cake-top edge, as shown. Pipe clangers (No.1).

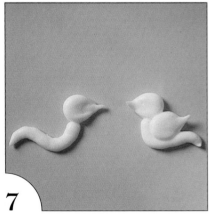

7
Pipe bird shapes around the cake-side (No.2).

8
Fix the ribbon ends to the cake-side to form loops, then pipe graduated dots as shown (No.1).

9
Pipe the floral motif shown around the cake-top edge (No.2). Decorate the cake with bells, ribbon loops and flowers of choice.

ROSALIE

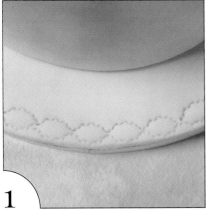

1
Cover the cake and board with sugarpaste. Immediately press holly patterned crimpers into the sugarpaste around the board edge, to form the design shown.

2
Pipe shells around the cake-base (No.43) with royal icing.

3
Gather together a selection of dried flowers, silk roses and leaves.

4
Make a large and small floral spray for the bottom and top tier together with two small sprays for the cake sides.

5
Fix the sprays to the cake-tops and narrow ribbons around the cake-sides.

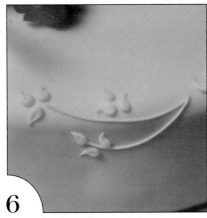

6
Pipe a floral motif around the remaining cake-top edge (No.1).

7
Pipe a floral motif onto the cake-top beside the back cake pillar (No.1).

8
Fix the small floral sprays to the cake-bases.

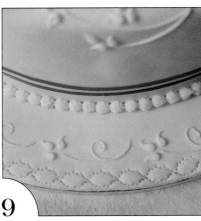

9
Pipe floral motifs around the cake boards (No.1). Fix banding around the cake boards.

PAM

1
Using a patterned scraper for the side, coat the cake with royal icing. When dry pipe bulbs around the cake-base (No.4).

2
Place a framed photograph and a spray of flowers onto the cake-top.

3
Pipe 'C' scrolls along the left side of the cake-top edge (No.3).

4
Pipe reversed 'C' scrolls along the right side of the cake-top edge (No.3).

5
Pipe dots, as shown, around the cake-side (No.1).

6
Pipe a leaf shape each side of the dots to complete the floral motifs (No.1).

7
Pipe 'C' and reversed 'C' scrolls onto the bulbs, using two colours in the piping bag (No.57).

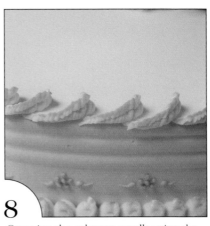

8
Overpipe the cake-top scrolls using the same colours and piping tube as in step 7.

9
Pipe message of choice and decorate in the manner shown (No.1).

SHEENA

1 Coat a cake with royal icing. Using the template as a guide cut out the various parts shown from sugarpaste.

2 When dry, place the parts together and decorate with ribbons and flower.

3 Fix bells and ribbons to the cake-top corner.

4 Fix numerals, then pipe message of choice (No.1) as shown.

5 Pipe scrolls around two sides of the cake-top edge (No.43).

6 Pipe shells around the remaining cake-top edge and base (No.43). Fix decorations of choice and ribbons around the cake-side and board.

TEMPLATES

PERLA

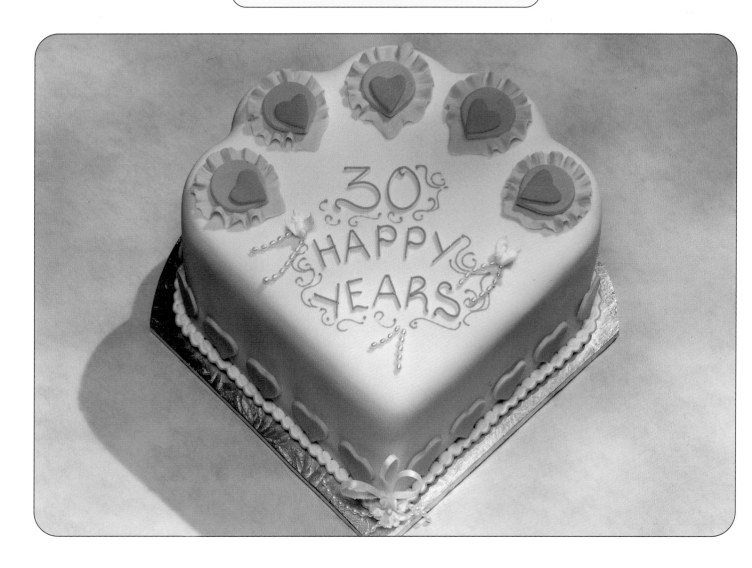

1 Cover a fan shaped cake with sugarpaste and place onto a shaped board. With royal icing, pipe shells around the cake-base (No.2).

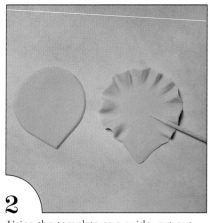

2 Using the template as a guide, cut out pear shapes from sugarpaste and frill the edges as shown.

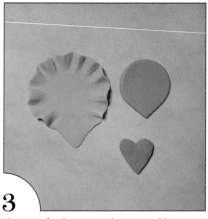

3 Cut out further pear shapes and hearts of reduced sizes.

4 Fix the shapes together and then fix to the cake-top.

5 Pipe a line over the shells (No.2).

6 Cut out and fix heart shapes, from sugarpaste, to the cake-side.

7 Make and fix ribbon sprays to the inner curves and cake-front.

8 Pipe inscription of choice (No.1) then overpipe the inscription (No.1).

9 Pipe tracery around the inscription (No.1) then fix matching decorations as shown.

TEMPLATES

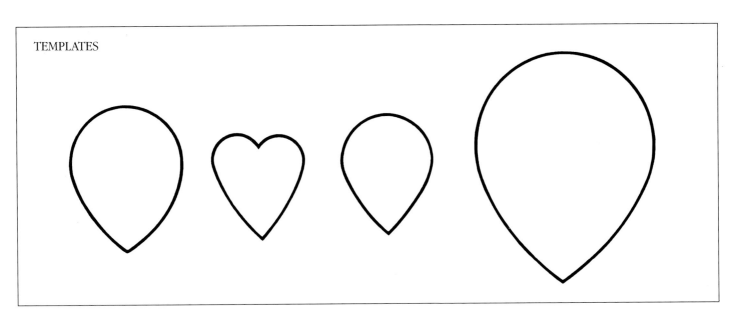

RUBY

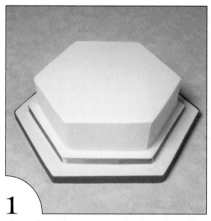

1 Coat the cake on two cake boards with royal icing. Leave to dry for 24 hours. Fix ribbon around each board edge.

2 Fix a ribbon band across the cake-top, then an appropriate motif. Pipe shells at each end (No.1).

3 Pipe inscription of choice (No.1) with royal icing. Fix numerals. Decorate with piped tracery (No.1).

4 Pipe the scrolls, as shown, onto the back edge of the cake-top (No.44).

5 Pipe the further scrolls as shown (No.44).

6 Pipe shells around the remaining cake-top edge and base (No.3).

7 Overpipe the scrolls (No.2). Then overpipe the No.2 line (No.1).

8 Pipe a line over the cake-base shells (No.2). Then overpipe the No.2 line (No.1).

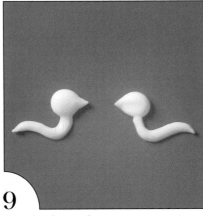

9 Pipe the shapes shown onto a practise board to form head and body of birds (No.2).

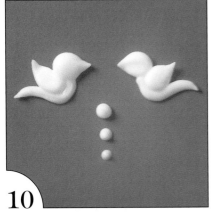

10 Pipe the wings and dots as shown (No.2). Then copy the design onto each side of the cake.

11 Pipe shells around the small cake board edge (No.2).

12 Pipe a scalloped line and dots around the edge of the large cake board. Fix flowers and leaves on each corner and onto the cake-top with a horseshoe.

ANNA

1
Coat the cake and board with royal icing, using a patterned scraper for the cake-side. Cut out and fix sugarpaste flowers around the cake-base.

2
Cut out and fix sugarpaste plaques to the cake-top and decorate with flowers. Pipe inscription of choice with royal icing.

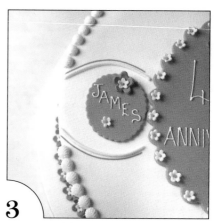

3
Pipe curved lines (No's.2 and 1) on the cake-top and shells around the edge (No.43). Fix ribbon around the cake board.

GOLDIE

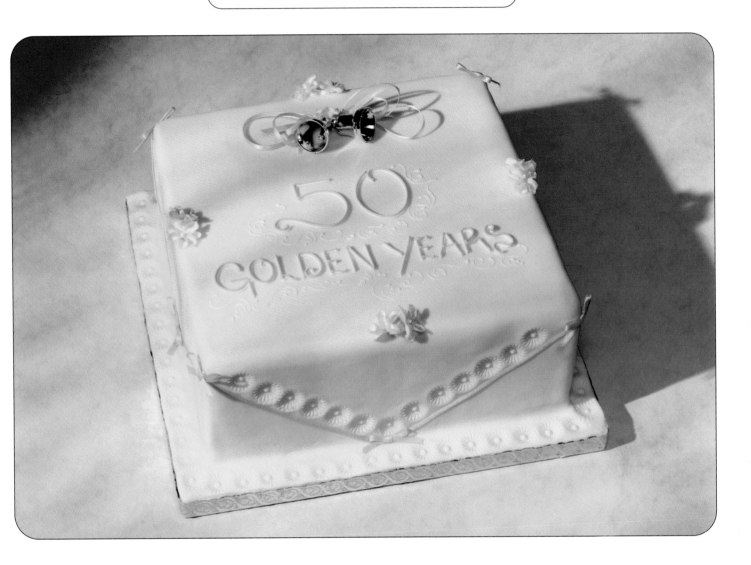

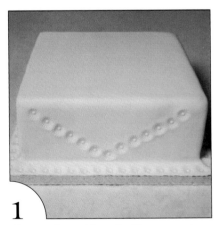

1
Cover cake and board with sugarpaste. Press a decorative button into the cake-sides and board to form the pattern shown.

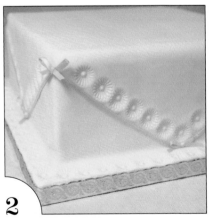

2
Fix ribbon and bows around the cake-sides.

3
Pipe inscription of choice, then tracery, with royal icing (No.1). Then decorate the cake-top with ribbons, flowers and bells.

1
Cover cake with sugarpaste. Using the template as a guide, cut out and fix sugarpaste pieces. Filigree the board with royal icing (No.1).

2
Cut out an appropriate size sugarpaste diamond. Crimp the edge. Pipe and decorate inscription of choice (No.1). Fix numerals as shown.

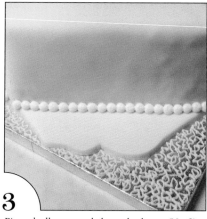

3
Pipe shells around the cake-base (No.2).

4 Fix the diamond plaque onto the cake-top and decorate with ribbon bows.

5 Pipe the lines shown around the cake-top edge, leaving a space at each corner (No.2). Pipe dots as shown (No.1).

6 Pipe a line over the shells (No.1). Fix flowers, leaves and ribbons as required.

TEMPLATES

KRISTA

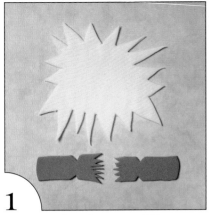

1 Using templates from page 187 as a guide, cut out sugarpaste shapes as shown.

2 Place the shapes onto the cake-top and pipe inscription of choice with royal icing (No.1).

3 Pipe scrolls and shells around the cake-top edge (No.43). Then pipe lines as shown (No.2). Fix decorations as required and band around the cake-side.

PANDORA

1 Cover the cake and board with sugarpaste. Cut two strips of sugarpaste and crimp along the centre line. Immediately fix the strips over the cake and board, as shown.

2 Pipe shells with royal icing (No.44) around the cake-base between the strips.

3 Pipe a leaf and berry on each shell as shown. Then fix appropriate seasonal decorations of choice.

WILMA

1 Using the template as a guide, cut out and fix sugarpaste fireplace pieces onto a cake coated with royal icing. Then mark the lines as shown.

2 Cut out and fix the further pieces shown and then mark the lines.

3 Cut out and fix sugarpaste socks, then decorate with royal icing (No.1).

4 Cut out and fix sugarpaste holly leaves. Pipe inscription of choice and berries (No.1).

5 Pipe scrolls and shells around the cake-top edge (No.44).

6 Pipe shells around the cake-base (No.44). Pipe a dot between each cake-base shell (No.1). Fix ribbon around the cake-side and board.

TEMPLATE

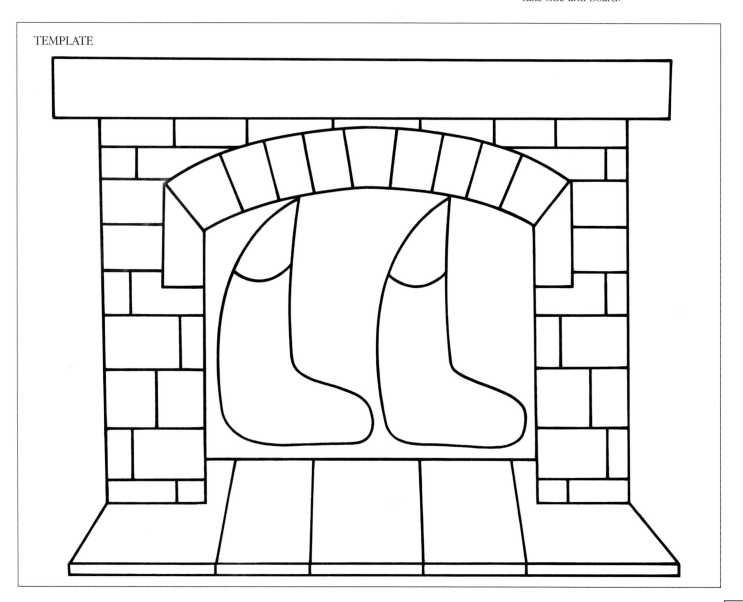

CHRISSIE

1 Cover a fan-shaped cake with sugarpaste.

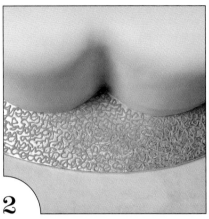

2 Filigree (No.1), or stipple the cake board with royal icing.

3 Pipe shells around the cake-base (No.3).

4 Pipe a line over the shells (No.2). Then overpipe the No.2 line (No.1).

5 Make and fix a floral spray to the cake-top corner.

6 Complete the spray, at the back of the cake, as shown.

7 Pipe message of choice onto the cake-top (No.1).

8 Pipe holly and berries between the message (No.1).

9 Pipe tracery, holly, berries and scrolls under the message (No.1). Fix ribbon bows as required.

1

Sugarpaste a cake and board in the shape shown. Crimp the sugarpaste around the board edge. Fix ribbons and centre decoration.

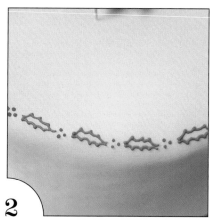

2

Pipe holly and berries around the cake-top edge and base, with royal icing (No.1).

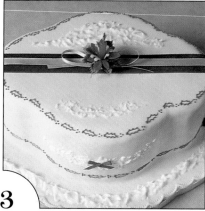

3

Stipple royal icing onto the cake-top, side and board using a small palette knife. Fix a ribbon bow to the back and front. Then fix band around the board edge.

1 Using templates from p.187 as a guide, cut out sugarpaste shapes as shown.

2 Fix the shapes onto the cake-top and decorate as shown. Pipe royal icing to form snow (No.2).

3 Mould sugarpaste into snowballs and fix around the cake-top edge. Fix band around the cake-side.

RUDOLPH

1 Cover an oval cake and board with sugarpaste. Stipple royal icing to form mountain scene on the cake-top, then stipple the cake-side and board.

2 Using templates as a guide, cut out sugarpaste reindeers and place onto non-stick paper. Leave until dry.

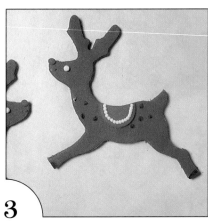

3 Cut out and fix a sugarpaste saddle to each reindeer. Using royal icing, decorate the reindeers as shown (No.1).

4 Cut out and fix sugarpaste stars and a moon to the cake-top.

5 Fix the reindeers as shown.

6 Cut out and fix a sugarpaste plaque. Then pipe message of choice (No.1). Fix ribbon around the cake board edge.

TEMPLATES

ST. NICHOLAS

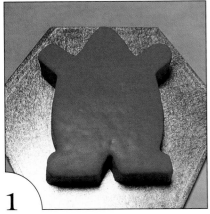

1

Using the template as a guide, cut-out the shape from sponge. Place onto an hexagonal board and cover sponge with sugarpaste.

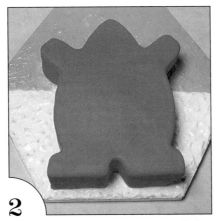

2

Stipple royal icing onto the top half of the board, using a household sponge. Then stipple lower half, using a palette knife.

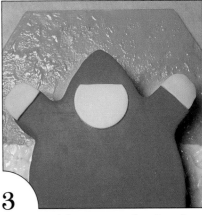

3

Cut-out and fix sugarpaste hands and face.

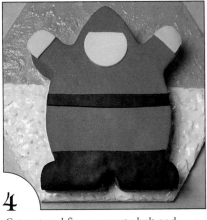

4

Cut-out and fix sugarpaste belt and boots.

5

Mould and fix sugarpaste nose and mouth. Pipe the eyes as shown with royal icing (No.2).

6

Spread royal icing with a paint brush to form the beard. Pipe eye brows (No.2). Pipe moustache, rope lines and rosette (No.6).

7

Roll out and fix sugarpaste trouser divide. Pipe rope lines as shown (No.6).

8

Pipe buttons (No.2) and buckle (No.1).

9

Cut-out and fix sugarpaste banner and decorate with Christmas message, bells and bows.

TEMPLATE

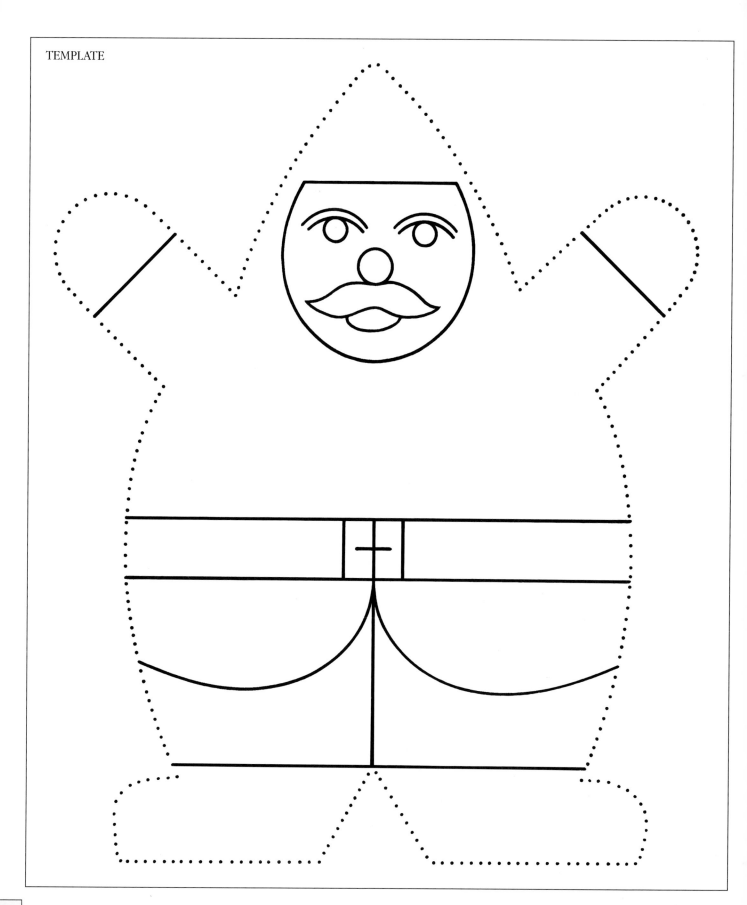

IVY

1 Cover a cake with sugarpaste and place onto a board. Spread royal icing around the board, using a comb-shaped scraper. Pipe shells (No.7) around the cake-base.

2 Pipe varying curved lines around the cake-top edge (No.2).

3 Cut out and fix sugarpaste holly and ivy leaves. Pipe berries (No.1). Fix seasonal decorations and ribbons as required.

PEACE

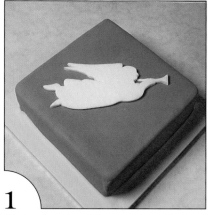

1 Cover the cake with sugarpaste. Then spread royal icing around the board edge. Using the templates as a guide, cut out and fix sugarpaste angel.

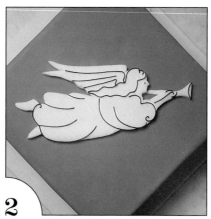

2 Pipe the lines shown with royal icing (No.1).

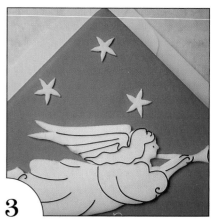

3 Cut out and fix sugarpaste star shapes onto the cake-top and sides.

4 Pipe inscription of choice and decorate with tracery (No.1).

5 Pipe curved rope lines around the cake-base (No.43).

6 Pipe curved lines beside the rope lines (No.2) then overpipe the lines (No.1). Fix leaves and flowers to the cake corners and a ribbon bow as shown.

TEMPLATE

JOYOUS

1

Coat a cake and board with royal icing, using a comb scraper for the cake-side. Leave to dry for 24 hours.

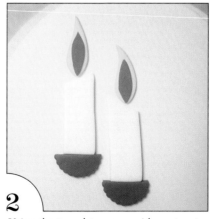

2

Using the templates as a guide, cut out sugarpaste candles and fix to the cake-top, as shown.

3

Fix sugarpaste, frilled with a cocktail stick, to the top and base of each candle.

4 Pipe the candle supports, lines and message of choice with royal icing (No's. 2 and 1).

5 Pipe scrolls around the cake-top edge (No.7). Then pipe the graduated dots (No.1).

6 Pipe spiral shells around the cake-base (No.7). Then pipe graduated dots on the cake board (No.1). Fix ribbons around the cake-side and board.

TEMPLATES

CHRISTOS

1 Layer cake or sponge into a square shape and cover with sugarpaste. Mark around the sides to form brick outlines.

2 Cover and fix two round cakes onto the top. Cut and fix a sugarpaste circle on each cake. Then stipple royal icing, as shown.

3 Fix festive decorations as required. Fix ribbon around the board edge.

TRISTAN

1 Cover a cake and board with sugarpaste. Cut out and fix the Christmas tree in the shape shown.

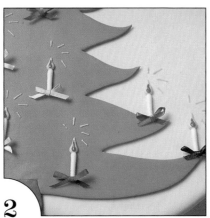

2 Pipe the candles with royal icing (No.3). Then pipe the light lines (No.1). Fix a ribbon bow to the base of each candle.

3 Pipe shells around the cake-base (No.43). Then pipe a line over the shells (No.2). Then overpipe the line (No.1). Fix motif of choice and ribbons as required.

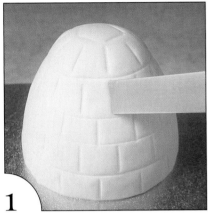

1

Cover a basin shaped sponge with
sugarpaste and place on a cake board.
Immediately mark to form the lines
shown.

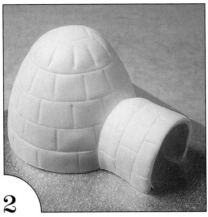

2

Make a sugarpaste entrance and fix to
the igloo, supported by a piece of card.

3

Cut and fix a flat, round piece of
sugarpaste for water hole. Then cut and
fix a sugarpaste block for a seat.

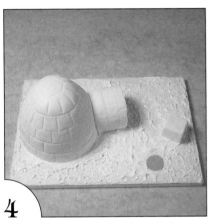

4

Stipple the remaining surface of the
board with royal icing.

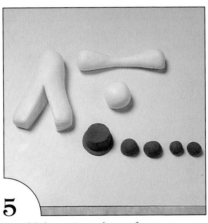

5

Mould the various shapes from
sugarpaste for the large snowman.

6

Assemble, and fix the snowman onto
the seat as shown.

7

Decorate the snowman with royal icing
(No.1). Make and fix a fishing rod using
spaghetti and thread. Make a sugarpaste
bucket of fish.

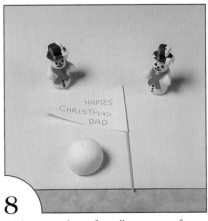

8

Make a number of small snowmen from
sugarpaste and decorate with royal icing
(No.1). Make a flag and sugarpaste base.

9

Fix the snowmen and flag as required.
Then decorate with seasonal sprays.

BELICIA

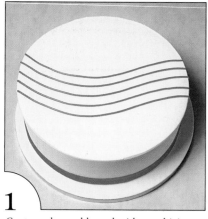

1 Coat a cake and board with royal icing. Leave to dry 24 hours. Fix ribbon around the cake-base. Using the template as a guide, pipe the lines shown (No.2).

2 Pipe the musical motif onto waxed paper (No.4). Leave until dry.

3 Remove the motif from the paper and fix to the cake-top. Pipe various musical notes (No.1).

4 Pipe shells around part of the cake-top edge (No.3) as shown.

5 Pipe musical notes around the cake-side (No.1).

6 Pipe inscription of choice onto the cake-top (No.1). Then fix seasonal decorations as required.

TEMPLATE

1 Coat a cake with royal icing, using a patterned scraper for the sides. Leave to dry for 24 hours.

2 Place a square of sugarpaste onto the cake-top and cut an upturned 'T' shape.

3 Carefully roll back the two flaps as shown.

4 Stipple royal icing around the cake-top edge.

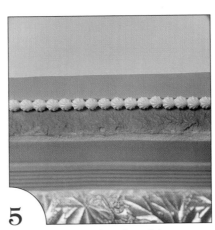

5 Pipe shells along the edge of the sugarpaste (No.42).

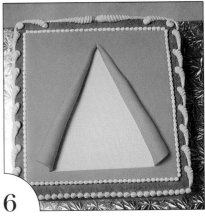

6 Pipe scrolls and shells around the cake-top edge (No.42).

7 Pipe message of choice and musical notes (No.1). Fix bells and ribbons at the cake-top.

8 Pipe shells around the cake-base (No.44).

9 Pipe a musical note onto a selection of cake-base shells (No.1). Fix decorations of choice.

INDEX AND GLOSSARY

Fix. To join
– Use apricot purée when fixing cake to cake or almond paste to cake.
– Use cooled boiled water or clear liquor when fixing sugarpaste to sugarpaste.
– Use royal icing when fixing to royal icing.
– Use royal icing when fixing run-outs, or piped figures, to royal icing or sugarpaste.
– Fix sugarpaste to buttercream by pressing it gently into the buttercream.
– Fix artificial decorations

Fix. To join continued
or modelling paste to sugarpaste, or royal icing, with royal icing.
– Fix ribbons with a small amount of royal icing.

Frills. To make frills, place tapered end of a cocktail stick over the edge of thinly rolled sugarpaste and rock it back and forth a little at a time.

Leave to dry for. Means leave to dry for (time stated) in a temperature of 18°C/65°F. Note: In high humidity a longer time may be needed.

Modelling paste. This is used for cut-out figures that need to stand alone as it is stronger than sugarpaste. Fix to cake-top with royal icing.

(No.1). This indicates the use of a Mary Ford No.1 piping tube (see p.207). Other bracketed numbers indicate the appropriate piping tubes to be used.

Overpipe. To repeat same pattern on existing piping.

Pipe-in. To pipe medium in use without a piping tube.

Runout. A runout is softened royal icing held in position with a piped line on waxed paper, or on the cake.
– drying, see – Leave to dry.

PIPING TUBE SHAPES

PIPING TUBE SHAPES

The diagram shows the icing tube shapes used in this book. Please note that these are Mary Ford tubes, but comparable tubes may be used. All the tools and equipment required to complete the cakes and decorations in this book are obtainable from local stockists.

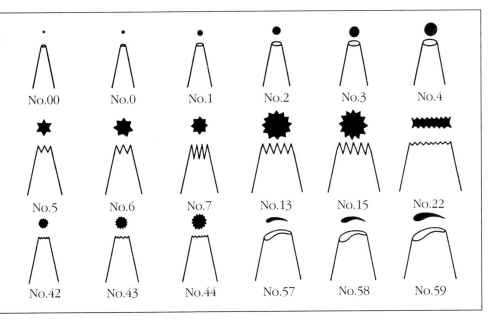

No.00　No.0　No.1　No.2　No.3　No.4

No.5　No.6　No.7　No.13　No.15　No.22

No.42　No.43　No.44　No.57　No.58　No.59

TIERING CAKES

For a 20.5cm (8") cake, pillars should be positioned 6.5cm (2½") from the centre. For a 25.5cm (10") cake, pillars should be positioned 7.5cm (3") from the centre. A square cake usually has 4 pillars which can be on the diagonal or cross, whichever suits the design best. A round cake usually has 3 pillars in a triangle, or four arranged in a circle.

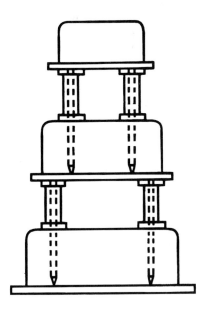

TIERING A SUGARPASTE-COVERED CAKE

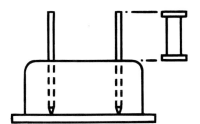

1
Push food-approved rods into the cake to the board. Cut rods to height of pillar.

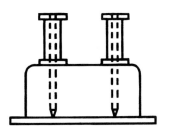

2
Place the pillars over the rods.

3
Assemble the cake, as required.

MARY FORD TITLES

101 Cake Designs

ISBN: 0 946429 00 6   320 pages
The original Mary Ford definitive cake artistry text book. A classic in its field, over 250,000 copies sold.

Cake Making and Decorating

ISBN: 0 946429 41 3   96 pages
Mary Ford divulges all the skills and techniques cake decorators need to make and decorate a variety of cakes in every medium.

Chocolate Cookbook

ISBN: 0 946429 18 9   96 pages
A complete introduction to cooking with chocolate featuring sweets, luscious gateaux, rich desserts and Easter Eggs.

Jams, Chutneys and Pickles

ISBN: 0 946429 33 2   96 pages
Over 70 of Mary Ford's favourite recipes for delicious jams, jellies, pickles and chutneys with hints and tips for perfect results.

Sugarpaste Cake Decorating

ISBN: 0 946429 10 3   96 pages
27 innovative Mary Ford cake designs illustrating royal icing decoration on sugarpaste covered cakes.

Children's Cakes

ISBN: 0 946429 35 9   96 pages
33 exciting new Mary Ford designs and templates for children's cakes in a wide range of mediums.

Party Cakes

ISBN: 0 946429 09 X   120 pages
36 superb party time sponge cake designs and templates for tots to teenagers. An invaluable prop for the party cake decorator.

Sugar Flowers Cake Decorating

ISBN: 0 946429 12 X   96 pages
Practical, easy-to-follow pictorial instructions for making and using superb, natural looking sugar flowers for cakes.

Decorative Sugar Flowers for Cakes

ISBN: 0 946429 28 6   120 pages
33 of the highest quality handcrafted sugar flowers with cutter shapes, background information and appropriate uses.

Sugarcraft Cake Decorating

ISBN: 0 946429 30 8   96 pages
A definitive sugarcraft book featuring an extensive selection of exquisite sugarcraft items designed and made by Pat Ashby.

Making Glove Puppets

ISBN: 0 946429 26 X   96 pages
14 specially designed fun glove puppets with full size templates and step-by-step instructions for each stage.

Home Baking with Chocolate

ISBN: 0 946429 37 5   96 pages
Over 60 tried and tested recipes for cakes, gateaux, biscuits, confectionery and desserts. The ideal book for busy mothers.

Desserts

ISBN: 0 946429 40 5   96 pages
Hot and cold desserts suitable for every occasion using fresh, natural ingredients. An invaluable reference book for the home cook, student or chef.

The Complete Book of Cake Decorating

ISBN: 0 946429 36 7   256 pages
An indispensable reference book for cake decorators, containing totally new material covering every aspect of cake design and artistry.

The Beginners Guide to Cake Decorating

ISBN: 0 946429 38 3   256 pages
A comprehensive guide for the complete beginner, to every stage of the cake decorating process, including over 150 cake designs for different occasions.